Praise for *The Productivity Chain*

"Get more work done faster than ever before—this book shows you how."
  Brian Tracy, author, Time Power

"Casey's book has not only helped me to be more productive in my business, I have also found it useful in my personal life. Whenever I'm stuck, I can refer to the book and figure out where the sticking point is and then apply the principles to move forward. My highest recommendation!"
  Tom Johnson, Owner, Altavista Recording

"Casey Moore is at her best in this book! She has made the complex simple, helping me to understand my problems, and see that the solutions already reside within me. Thank you for helping to change my perspective of the age-old problems of 'disorganization' and 'time management.'"
  Eddie Drescher, Business Consultant, Virginia Beach

"What a refreshing perspective on a subject in which we tend to spin our wheels. Instead of creating a new-fangled method for organizing, Casey gets deep into your head, clarifying what factors will truly boost your productivity. Her book reads like confessions of her real clients—we relate and draw hope because we find ourselves in them.

  "Casey has real-world knowledge and experience and shares deeply from her work. Warning—you may not like this book if you are unwilling to get a clear look at the failing elements of your life that are in desperate need of change. If you listen to her wisdom, however, you will find a new level of performance in your future."
  Hillery R. Schanck, CIMA, Financial Advisor, Virginia Beach

"Casey nails it! This book is loaded with clear, simple, practical ideas and real-life examples of how to go from ineffective and inefficient to productive and powerful. **The Productivity Chain is THE roadmap to success and the next must-**have assessment tool."
  Patty Kreamer, CPO®, author, But I Might Need It Someday!

"[This book] provides a practical, prescriptive approach to understanding productivity. The Productivity Chain creates a model that achieves 'simplicity without simplification.' This book is ideal for anyone who wants to stop making excuses and start taking real action."

    Lisa Renz, author, My Life on One Road

"The model Casey has designed to assist us in understanding productivity and effectiveness is both creative and accessible. It cuts through familiar territory with fresh intelligence and common sense. Everyone will be able to use her perspective and strategies to great advantage."

    Denslow Brown, MCC, CPO®, CPO-CD®, author,
    Processing Modalities Guide

"Well-written and organized...I really relate to the Productivity Chain. I was completely absorbed."

    Peggy Jenkins, Project Manager, Austin

"Over and over, I see very talented, driven and organized people fail. They were efficient yet not effective because, at the end of the day, they were not productive. Casey Moore could have helped those people. They were so close to real, purposeful and satisfying success...but didn't know the lessons she is now teaching others."

    Gary Corless, CEO, PSS World Medical, Inc.

"I always worked hard but my projects still seemed to pile up. I could never understand why my high degree of capability did not automatically translate into a high degree of productivity. Casey taught me it's not **how much** you work, but **how** you work that makes all the difference.

"She changed my life by making that connection for me and helping me change my approach. Now, I spend fewer hours at the office—yet get more work done—because I apply the concepts described in this book. I got to learn them firsthand. Thank you, Casey, for teaching me the true joys of a productive life!"

    C. Arthur " Brother" Rutter III, attorney, Rutter Mills, LLP

The Holistic Way
to Spend Your Time
on What Matters

THE PRODUCTIVITY CHAIN

Stop Organizing, Start Producing – Second Edition

Casey Moore, PCC, CPO®, PCOC

Worksong Publishing
Chesapeake, Virginia

Worksong Publishing

Copyright © 2018 by (Elizabeth) Casey Moore. All rights reserved.

The author's permission is required to reproduce or distribute any part of this book in any form, printed or electronic. Please purchase only authorized editions.

Cover design: Holly Wolfe of Wolfe Design Studio
Cover photo (author): Judith Soule, Virginia Beach, Virginia
Cover fronto (front): BigStock.com

The Library of Congress has catalogued this book as follows:
Control Number: 2017911627
Moore, Casey
The Productivity Chain: Spend Your Time on What Matters

ISBN: 978-0-692-90523-4

PRINTED IN THE UNITED STATES OF AMERICA

Acknowledgements

Mark
for your persevering love, encouragement, and support

This book has been a long time in the making. It took a village to complete and update. My heartfelt thanks to...

...my wonderful clients from over the past two decades—you've taught me so much and I've been honored to share your journeys; my loyal eTip recipients; the Circle of Excellence group; my fellow Coach Approach for Organizers coaches and NAPO comrades; and my family and friends.

...those who shared their feedback and/or gave their permission for their ideas to be included in this edition of the book: Barbara Hemphill, Brian Tracy, Brother Rutter, Chris Kettner, David Allen, Denslow Brown, Eddie Drescher, Gary Corless, Hillery Schanck, Judith Kolberg, Lisa Renz, Patty Kreamer, Peggy Jenkins, Tom Johnson, and Dr. Stephen Covey. Special thanks to Debbie Bowie and Dr. Avi Santo for encouraging me to expand on the concept of Context.

...the experts who contributed to this work: Melissa Saphir (editing, channeling, and midwifery); Annie Hartnett of Artemis Editorial (initial editing and advising); Holly Wolfe of Wolfe Design Studio (graphic design); Deborah Data Group (transcription); Marshall McClure of MarshallArts (early proofreading); Judith Soule (photography); and Tom Noffsinger of R2R Marketing (website design).

Table of Contents

Acknowledgements...iii
Preface...vii
Introduction...ix
How to Use This Book...xiv
The Summary...xvi

Section I: The Productivity Chain

Introduction...1
1: A New Productivity Model...3
2: How the Productivity Chain Functions...12
3: A Powerful Perspective...18
4: Identify Solutions (The Productivity Chain Analysis)...24
5: Strengthen Your Weak Links...33
6: The Power Chain...37
7: A Guiding Framework...43
Your Next Step...46
Case Study: Douglas...47

Section II: The Twelve Links

Introduction...53
8: Boundary-setting...55
9: Communication/Relationships...61
10: Decision-making...70
11: Delegation...76
12: Drive...82
13: Goal-setting/Prioritization...89
14: Health...97
15: Organization of Objects/Data...106
16: Planning...115

17: Reinvention...124
18: Resources...131
19: Task/Project Management...137
Your Next Step...144
Case Study: Butch...145

Section III: Productivity Myths

Introduction...149
20: Overcome Your Productivity Myths...152
21: I Can Do It All...154
22: I Need More Time...160
23: I Need to Work Harder...164
24: I Need to Get More Organized...169
25: I Should Be Able to Handle Everything Myself...175
26: I Can Make Up for Lost Time...178
27: I Can't Play Until My Work Is Done...184
28: I Am Not Naturally Productive...187
29: Others Can Make Up for What I Lack...191
30: Other People Are the Problem...196
31: My Productivity Problem Has No Upside...203
32: The Problem Will Get Better by Itself...208
Case Study: Karen...213

Afterword...216

Appendix

A: Productivity Chain Self-Assessment...219
B: Instant Reframe Examples...220
C: Productivity-Related Terms...223
D: Productivity-Related Resources...229
E: Endnotes...231

Index...235

Preface: Mindfulness Magic

It's been a number of years since I wrote *Stop Organizing, Start Producing*. The worlds of work and personal life—if the distinction still applies—have only gotten busier. Still, the Productivity Chain Model continues to accurately and helpfully depict how personal productivity occurs and how you can influence it. Given the seeming increase in demands on our time, the ever-expanding sources of distraction, and the over-abundance of choice options for even minor decisions, a simple model that clarifies what helps you achieve your goals is vital. It applies whether you want to "produce" top performance at work or a relaxing evening at home.

For that reason, I've kept the book largely as it was. The major exception is the addition of this preface and some updates to Section I and the Appendices.

Understandably, people have always clamored for a productivity "magic bullet" that could solve their problems and make them instantly more effective and efficient. For years, I counseled my clients, workshop participants, and readers that no such habit or tool existed. Since the first edition of the book, however, I have changed my mind. Practicing mindfulness, while not an instant remedy, is a habit that almost magically boosts your productivity.

Mindfulness has many definitions. Essentially, it involves paying attention purposefully and non-judgmentally in the present moment. That attention may rest on what is happening within your mind, body, or environment. If practiced consistently, mindfulness almost inevitably yields greater productivity, along with a host of other positive effects on mood, outlook, health, and relationships.[1] Describing all the gifts of mindfulness would fill another book, so

I'll stop here. My experience, and that of others, is that the more mindfulness is practiced, the greater these rewards.

Why these amazing results? Practicing mindfulness actually reshapes brain structures, achieved through your brain's neuroplasticity.[2] To learn more about the neurology involved, I recommend reading *Rewire Your Brain for Love* by Marsha Lucas, Ph.D. She is a clinical psychologist who explains the science in everyday language.

Mindfulness' positive impact on productivity is easy to understand. Its non-judgmental awareness boosts every individual link in the Productivity Chain. Practicing mindfulness has been shown, for example, to increase the size of the hippocampus, which is associated with learning, memory, self-awareness, and compassion.[3] An improved ability to learn strengthens your Resources and Reinvention links. Greater self-awareness and compassion, meanwhile, fortify your Boundary-setting and Communication/Relationships links. The very act of practicing mindfulness enhances your ability to focus and let go of distractions, strengthening your Drive link. The list could go on.

Because it enhances all twelve links in the Chain, mindfulness is a practice I highly encourage you to begin immediately. Even just a few minutes a day can make a difference. When you experience the benefits, you may find yourself devoting more time to it. Notice how it affects your decision-making, relationships, self-care, and more. I think you will find, as I have observed in myself and in my clients, that mindfulness is a powerful support for you as you apply the ideas in this book to your daily life.

Introduction

Life is short and precious.

We have only so much time to contribute to the world through our work. We often have even less time to spend with those we love. Learning to make the best use of our limited time—to match our actions with our values—may be the most important skill set we can develop.

That learning itself should be as efficient and effective as possible. We can't afford to waste time trying just any tool or technique that promises to "fix" our approach to work and time. We need solutions targeted to meet our specific needs and goals. As we apply them, we can be of greater service at work and more present in our lives outside it.

Wasting Time Trying to Save Time

Unfortunately, many people *do* waste trying to improve their "time management." They keep trying to fix what isn't broken. You may be one of them. You know or suspect that you could perform at a higher level, but you aren't sure how. You assume that if you were "more organized," your results would improve. But what does "more organized" mean?

People talk about "organizing" their thoughts, systems, communication, employees, priorities, papers, projects, emails, relationships, schedules, and lives...We use the word so often, in so many contexts, that it has become almost meaningless.

That's why getting "more organized" usually fails. It's why I wrote the first edition of this book, which was titled *Stop Organizing, Start Producing*. If you are like most people, being organized is just a means to an end. What you really want is to be

THE PRODUCTIVITY CHAIN

> You want to feel more in control of your time and your life. That's a reasonable and achievable desire.

more **productive**. You want to feel more in control of your time and your life, or at least more intentional about how you spend it. That's a reasonable and achievable desire. This book will help you do just that.

No one can *make* you spend your time more wisely. This book, however, will show you how to figure out what gets in your way. By correctly "diagnosing" your problem, you automatically identify its solution. You understand exactly what you need to do to achieve your goals—whether you want to shatter sales records, spend more time with your family, or both.

Immediately, your perspective improves. Just understanding the many complex factors that determine your personal productivity is helpful. Whether you act on what you learn or not, you will feel a greater sense of power and control. If you often feel "at the mercy" of your phone, email, or other people, regaining that power means a lot.

A More Productive View

Type "productivity" into a search engine and you will find hundreds of millions of books, videos, sites, articles, and experts on the topic. Most focus on one or two narrow aspects of productivity. They discuss getting physically organized, managing time, communicating effectively, or managing others, for example.

It helps to study these issues in depth. But it is **vital** to step back and look at the bigger picture first—to understand how these topics interrelate and to determine which contribute to **your** productivity problems. Then your study can be faster and focused.

That's what this book does. It offers a comprehensive model for productivity that empowers you to make significant, lasting improvements in your work performance. It helps you strategically address the core factors that keep you from functioning as powerfully or as effortlessly as you would like.

This model is the Productivity Chain.® The links in the Chain are the twelve factors that determine how productive you can be at any given time (see box).

Examining your Productivity Chain's strengths and weaknesses enables you to perform laser surgery to improve your work habits,

INTRODUCTION

> **Links in the Productivity Chain**
>
> These twelve factors determine how productive you can be:
> - Boundary-setting
> - Communication/Relationships
> - Decision-making
> - Delegation
> - Drive
> - Goal-setting/Prioritization
> - Health
> - Resources
> - Organization of Objects/Data
> - Planning
> - Reinvention
> - Task/Project Management

rather than going in with a chainsaw. You don't have to overhaul every behavior or change your entire life. Just identify the weak links in your Chain and develop practices to strengthen them.

By making your weak areas just strong enough so they no longer undermine your real strengths, you increase your productivity overall. Your stress diminishes. Your quality of life and work improves. Best of all, the improvements last because they stem from your developing specific, concrete habits and skills.

My Story

The Productivity Chain model has certainly helped me. I became a Professional Organizer in 2000, but soon realized that getting organized wasn't enough to help my clients achieve the performance—or lives—they wanted. By 2004, I had developed the Productivity Chain model and called myself a Productivity Trainer and, eventually, Coach. Over my career, I've helped so many people improve their performance and experience greater peace of mind at work. First, though, I had to help myself.

I was not always a productive or organized person. As a child, my parents often had to force me to clean my messy room. As a teen, I was a packrat, keeping all sorts of minutia as "memories."

Gradually, though, I began to like organizing my objects and information. I helped shape my identity by selecting what to toss and what to keep. Today, I still enjoy creating order out of chaos. It satisfies my soul.

It took longer for me to become more productive. Though I loved learning, my study habits were inefficient and often counterproductive. I endured plenty of all-nighters to get my good grades. Still, my interest in productivity began early. In seventh grade, I read a story about a man who was an efficiency expert and was enthralled. Doing things "better, faster, smarter" became my passion, but I didn't always know how.

Over time, through trial and error, I learned. Long before I gave my ideas a name, the Productivity Chain concept helped me. I saw the value in understanding my strengths and weaknesses. I understood the power of pinpointing my productivity problems, and addressing them with small, progressive changes.

My most damaging weakness was procrastination, an occupational hazard for many writers. In my former life as a career development researcher and author, I once produced a guide for the State of Texas that featured a special-topic page on procrastination. It was the last page of the book I wrote!

Awareness and acceptance of the weak links in my Productivity Chain keep them from hurting me today. If I do get stuck, I don't stay stuck for long. I recognize the problem and take action. Talking with a friend or getting a little coaching snaps me out of it fast. If the Productivity Chain can turn the Princess of Procrastination into the Queen of Completion, it can help you, too!

Learning to work and live ever more effectively is a lifelong effort. It has been for me. In 2007, I became one of the first Certified Professional Organizers® in the U.S.

Since then, I have continued my training. My study of special issues (such as Chronic Disorganization and Attention Deficit Disorder) and methods (such as coaching) better equip me to help others achieve their productivity goals. I practice what I learn so I can keep improving and speak from experience. I study hard so my clients won't have to.

> Learning to work and live ever more effectively is a lifelong effort.

Writing this book has fueled my commitment to cut through the hype about "getting organized," shed light on harmful myths, and share with fellow travelers some of the powerful productivity principles I have discovered, enjoyed, forgotten, and recovered over the years.

INTRODUCTION

Who This Book Is For

This book is for anyone who wants to accomplish more without sacrificing quality of life. It is for *you*.

My clients include CEOs, executives, salespeople, small business owners, attorneys, and other professionals, as well as some stay-at-home parents who run the "business" of their families and volunteer activities. What they have in common is a desire to use their time more wisely, achieve their goals more easily, and live more fully. The Productivity Chain has helped them—and it will help you, too.

My Promise to You

Will you be as productive as humanly possible every day from now on once you read this book? No. Will you become perfect by applying its ideas? No. But you *will* increase your desired output and you *will* learn how to grow ever more productive if you act on what you read.

Best of all, you will regain your sense of power and control over your work and time. Your days will not get "hijacked" by email and other external factors. You will find greater peace of mind.

This book is practical. It empowers you to think and act. If you follow its suggestions, you will improve your situation, whatever it is. You will regain your perspective about what matters at work and in your life. You will get more of the important things done and worry less about the rest. You will make better choices with your time.

> Your days will not get "hijacked" by email and other external factors. You will find greater peace of mind.

And if you stumble into a rough patch, and feel lost and alone in the valley of Overwhelmed or There's-Got-to-Be-a-Better-Way, the Productivity Chain will pull you back to the land of Power, Clarity, and Peace.

# How to Use this Book

This is your book. Do with it as you wish. To benefit most from it, however, here are some suggestions:

Read It <u>Your</u> Way

Each chapter is designed to be fairly stand-alone except for its references to the Productivity Chain. You can start at the beginning, middle, or end and gain simple, useful ideas and strategies to improve your work performance.

Section I explains the Productivity Chain, its functions, and its benefits. Section II explores the links of the Chain in greater depth. Section III debunks some of the myths that get in the way of your productivity.

If you read the book from cover to cover, you will find some repetition of key concepts, which will help you retain the ideas and put them to use.

Be open-minded about which chapters you select. You may want to skip certain productivity myths, for example, thinking they do not apply to you. Embedded within each, however, you will find valuable ideas and practices that may help you.

Identify with the People

Examples, stories, quotes, and case studies pepper the book. Try to identify with these people, almost all of whom are my clients. The more deeply you relate, the more successfully you can benefit from their experiences.

Their names and other identifying information have been changed to protect their confidentiality. Some are composites for

HOW TO USE THIS BOOK

the same reason. Most of the quotes come from interviews I did with clients in preparation for this book.

Do the Exercises and Take the Actions

To make positive changes in your life, complete the exercises and take the action recommendations sprinkled throughout the book. Treat it like a cookbook: You have to try out the recipes to judge its worth—and to satisfy your hunger for change.

The exercises can increase your clarity and, ultimately, your productivity. Most take only a few minutes, but they greatly enhance the value you get from this book.

Doing the exercises with a friend can be especially useful. It provides structure, accountability, and support. You may find it quite interesting, too. You can learn from each other's insights and experiences, especially as you put the book's ideas into practice in your daily life.

Apply It to Your Life

As you read, think about how the ideas and suggestions apply to your own situation. How can you translate a given example to your own experience? When the text asks you a direct question, stop and answer it, if only in your head. The more you bring yourself into the reading, the more relevant and applicable the ideas become.

Most of all, practice the suggestions in your daily life, starting today. Every chapter offers tips and strategies. They are not always labeled as such. A quote from someone might include a concept you can use.

The more effort you put into the change process, the more you will get out of it. One new habit of behavior beats five great ideas.

Re-read It

Read, skim, and re-read this book. Keep it as a reference. Some of its ideas may be new and take a while to sink in. The more you study and think about them, however, the more effectively you can apply them to your own life.

The Summary

Here is *The Productivity Chain* in short:

- There are twelve factors that determine your productivity level—twelve links in your Productivity Chain. (See Section II: *The Twelve Links*.)
- The links connect with and influence each other. You can only be as productive as your weakest link allows, regardless of how strong your other links may be. You can leverage improvements in one link to strengthen your entire Chain, increasing your overall productivity. (See Section I: *The Productivity Chain*.)
- The Chain enables you to accurately assess what keeps you from optimal performance. You can then target those exact areas to improve. You enhance your overall performance—and you do it quickly and efficiently. (See Section I: *The Productivity Chain*.)
- The Chain concept blows the lid off commonly held "myths" about productivity and time, such as "I need to get more organized" and "I need more time"—beliefs that keep you stuck at your current performance level. The Chain replaces them with a more realistic and empowering perspective. (See Section III: *Productivity Myths*.)
- The Chain and this book are really about personal power—how it helps, how to apply it, and how to keep it. A hidden source of your stress is giving away your power to technology (e.g., email), unrealistic expectations, other people, and your work itself. The Productivity Chain turns that around. The results: greater productivity, sense of control, and peace of mind.

If you stop here, I hope you've gained something useful. If you are intrigued, however, read on...

Section I
The Productivity Chain

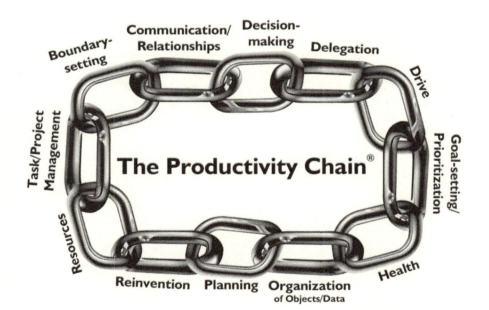

The Productivity Chain
Introduction

"Things do not change. We change."
—Henry David Thoreau

Carol called me while driving to her next appointment. Her voice was warm but tired. After twenty years at the top of her profession, she wanted a change.

"What made you call now?" I wondered.

"I just need to get more organized," she replied. "I've got so much on my plate, I don't have time for it all." As she described her work situation and the many offices and people she supervised, she tried to make sense of what was wrong. "I am organized," she admitted at one point, sounding confused. "I can find everything I need—I'm known for that. But I still feel overwhelmed."

No wonder she was confused. Conventional wisdom says being overwhelmed is a sign of disorganization. But if Carol is fairly organized already, what is the problem? And how can she fix it?

She can begin by forgetting conventional wisdom. Our cultural obsession with organization endures despite the fact that "organizing" doesn't deliver what most people really need: more productivity, greater sense of control, and less stress.

"Organizing" Doesn't Work

Conventional "organizing" can't produce those desired results because:

- **"Organizing" confuses ends with means.** People think organizing is the same as producing desired results. It is not. Too much organizing can even be counterproductive.

THE PRODUCTIVITY CHAIN

- **"Organizing" is too vague a term.** When pressed, people define "organizing" as everything from cleaning your desk to managing projects effectively. If it means so many things, how do you know what to change to improve your performance or, in Carol's case, to stop feeling overwhelmed?
- **"Organizing" wastes time.** When you don't know exactly what gets in your way—and therefore how to overcome it—you spend too much time in the problem. You spin your wheels, as Carol has done, or you put effort into solutions that won't help, such as re-organizing an already-organized office.

It's time for a more effective approach to work and life. It's called the Productivity Chain.

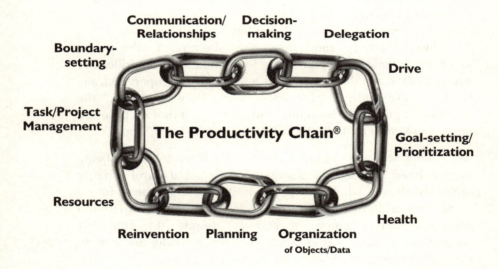

1 A New Productivity Model

"The Productivity Chain helped me deal with a manageable piece—rather than the whole picture—at one time. I'd still be frazzled if I had to deal with the whole thing at once."
—Joshua, CEO, manufacturing firm

The Productivity Chain offers a new way to understand what you need to achieve and maintain top performance. It redefines your productivity problems as weaknesses in specific links in your Chain, then identifies practical solutions to address those areas. This model enables you to improve quickly and successfully—especially compared to revamping your entire way of working or vaguely trying to "get organized."

Applying this practical model empowers you to view your work and world with new eyes. It shatters common myths about what prevents you from functioning as effectively as possible, freeing you to achieve your goals. Ultimately, it helps you live the life you really want, both inside and outside the office.

Twelve Factors Determine Your Productivity

Sounds promising, but how does it work? First, the Productivity Chain defines the twelve distinct factors that determine the level of productivity you—or anyone—can achieve.

Each factor—each link in the Chain—represents a set of skills, knowledge, and abilities that contributes to your performance. The names and functions of the links are (in alphabetical order):

1. **Boundary-setting:** Protects you and your time, energy, and other resources. It includes managing interruptions and commitments.

2. **Communication/Relationships:** Connects you to other people and their resources. It includes assertiveness, listening, kindness, and respect.
3. **Decision-making:** Activates your other links, and therefore your work itself. It includes problem-solving.
4. **Delegation:** Values you and your time by freeing you to work on your high-worth activities, while others help with the rest. (Delegation does not require an assistant or staff.)
5. **Drive:** Propels you and your work forward. It encompasses your motivation, attitude, and effort.
6. **Goal-setting/Prioritization:** Guides you and your work. It includes your—and your organization's—mission, purpose, values, needs, and so on.
7. **Health:** Energizes you by supplying the fuel and balance needed for top performance. It includes your physical, mental, emotional, social, and spiritual well-being.
8. **Organization of Objects/Data:** Economizes your work by enabling you to find the things and information you need as quickly and effortlessly as possible.
9. **Planning:** Operationalizes your work, especially by connecting your goals and expectations with the reality of time through scheduling.
10. **Reinvention:** Adapts you to change, whether the change involves shifting external conditions or evolving internal ones. It includes flexibility and resilience.
11. **Resources:** Equips you with the tools you need to do your work most effectively and efficiently. It includes self-knowledge, job-related knowledge and skills, organizational resources, and so on.
12. **Task/Project Management:** Advances your work one task and one project at a time. A "project" in this context refers to any goal or role that requires multiple steps to achieve.[1]

You can see the Productivity Chain labeled with key words on the next page. To learn more about the links, read Section II: *The*

1: A NEW PRODUCTIVITY MODEL

The Productivity Chain Model

The Productivity Chain has twelve links. The name of each link (below) is bolded, with the role it plays in your productivity in italics beneath it. To learn about the links in detail, see Section II: *The Twelve Links*.

Key Principles:
- You can only be as productive as your weakest link allows.
- Strengthen that link and your entire Chain gets stronger.

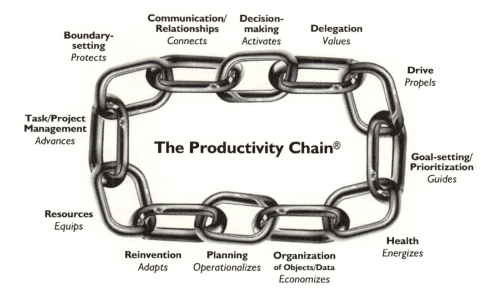

Twelve Links. Chapter 7: *A Guiding Framework* and Appendix C: *Productivity-Related Terms* identify where factors such as intelligence fit in the Chain.

The Whole Matters More than the Parts

Like links in a chain—your Productivity Chain—these twelve factors connect to and influence each other. Each contributes to your overall performance, but it is their **interaction** that determines how consistently productive you can be.

THE PRODUCTIVITY CHAIN

> ### Why a "Chain?"
>
> The twelve factors that determine your productivity are complex, multi-faceted, and ever-changing. They interrelate in ways far more intricate than strands in a spider's web. The Productivity Chain model expresses key aspects of this complexity through a familiar image you can see and touch.
>
> The chain metaphor is simple, yet still conveys three crucial truths: You have relative strengths and weaknesses. Your weaknesses constrain your overall effectiveness. Making even small improvements to those links greatly improves your Chain's overall strength and your productivity.
>
> Some people hear "chain" and think "limits." Chains can be used as restraints, of course, but they also support and protect. Far from tying you down, the Productivity Chain actually frees you from wasting your time trying to "fix" what isn't broken by identifying your weak links so you can target only them.
>
> The chain metaphor applies for other reasons, as well. A "chain" is a set of things with a logical connection[2]—which is what the twelve links really are. They are not unrelated bullet points or steps in a process. They interconnect.
>
> By definition, a "chain" also conveys power.[2] The Productivity Chain concept empowers you—offering a new perspective that enables you to take forceful action to improve your effectiveness.

As with any chain, your Productivity Chain is only as strong as its weakest link. A link may be weak because the necessary skills, knowledge, and abilities are missing, under-developed, or not applied. Weakness in just one area can cripple your total output, just as one broken link makes even the thickest steel chain useless.

In this model, every productivity problem—from too much work to coping poorly with change—has a simple cause: a weak link in your Chain. Fortunately, every solution is equally simple—identify and strengthen that weak link.

Strengthening a link not only improves that area; it reinforces the entire Chain, taking your overall effectiveness to a higher level. The stronger your links in general, with minimal undermining weaknesses, the higher and more sustainable your productivity.

1: A NEW PRODUCTIVITY MODEL

No one stays "in the zone" all the time, but you can increase your average so you get there more often and more easily. (To learn more, see Chapter 6: *The Power Chain*.)

The Chain Begins with "Productivity"

"Productivity is clearly knowing what you have to accomplish, the amount of time you have to accomplish it in, and then producing what you need in that time."
—Valarie, university professor

The Productivity Chain is a model for producing the outcomes you desire, whether that means achieving work-related goals or making the highest and best use of your time anywhere. It's not the "Work Chain" because your work itself doesn't matter. Your results do.

Results are what you ultimately produce, and they depend on your role. CEOs produce vision, leadership, and ultimately the continued growth and well-being of their organizations. Litigation attorneys produce depositions, interrogatory responses, and ultimately win cases. Salespeople produce prospects, quotes, and ultimately closed deals.

> **TAKE ACTION**
> Write down your responses: What do you ultimately produce that makes you valuable at work? How much do you produce?

What do you **ultimately** produce (or at least hope to)? What do you **actually** produce? The gap between the two measures your productivity problem or aspirations.

In the workplace, only the "ultimate" results matter. You might be great at the activities of an attorney who earns contingency fees, for example—the reading, writing, and negotiating. If you do not produce sufficient awards or settlements, however, you will not last—no matter how brilliant your legal analysis. Fortunately, the Productivity Chain helps you achieve results—productivity, not just activity.

Why "Stop Organizing" When Organization Is a Link in the Chain?

This book was originally called *Stop Organizing, Start Producing*, yet organization is a link in the Chain—a crucial link. You do

THE PRODUCTIVITY CHAIN

> The Productivity Chain helps you achieve productivity, not just activity.

function much more efficiently when you can quickly access the tools and information you need when you need them.

The link is actually called "Organization of Objects/Data," however, a label that narrowly defines what "organized" means in the Productivity Chain model. You are "organized" when you keep the objects in your office—such as documents, pens, and so on—where they occupy space efficiently and you can reach them easily. You are "organized" when you store your digital data—such as emails, files, and ideas—so you can access them quickly. (See Chapter 15: *Organization of Objects/Data*.)

If organizing objects and data is important, why should you stop doing it? You shouldn't stop completely, of course. Just limit it to what is necessary.

"Stop Organizing" really means:

1. **Stop saying "organized" when you mean "productive."** Focusing on productivity helps you move beyond organizing to see what other factors might contribute to both your problems and solutions. It helps you apply the Productivity Chain, in other words. By viewing your situation holistically, you hone in on specific problems and identify targeted, effective solutions.

2. **Stop trying to get more organized if you're organized enough.** It wastes time and effort. Some highly organized people are the least productive because they waste their time organizing instead of working or addressing the true causes of their productivity struggles. (See Myth Chapter 24: *I Need to Get More Organized* for details.)

When you change your mindset and vocabulary from "organized" to "productive" and use the Productivity Chain to define your terms even further, you move closer to becoming more productive because your path to it becomes clearer.

Carol's Chain Experience

That's what Carol did. She examined the links in her Productivity Chain one by one, looking for her strengths and weaknesses. Since

1: A NEW PRODUCTIVITY MODEL

Organization of Objects/Data usually fell in her "strong" category, she realized that other factors were responsible for making her feel overwhelmed. Getting more organized would not change them.

It took her a little while to reach this conclusion because recently her office had become a bit cluttered. Looking at the big picture of the Chain, though, convinced her to view the stacks as symptoms, rather than causes. She had strong organizational skills but had not applied them. It was a matter of priorities. Forced to choose between filing and making money, Carol chose the latter. (Her Goal-setting/Prioritization link was strong.)

Feeling she **had** to choose between the two was another symptom of Carol's real productivity problem—having too much on her plate. Poor boundary-setting had led her to take on too many responsibilities at work and volunteer commitments in her personal life. Lack of delegation kept those assignments on her desk. These factors temporarily weakened her Organization of Objects/Data link.

> Carol's real productivity problem was having too much on her plate because of weak Boundary-setting and Delegation links.

Carol began practicing the precise behaviors and attitudes that would strengthen her weak links. She said "no," "not now," and "I trust you to handle it yourself" to avoid taking on too much and to manage interruptions (Boundary-setting link). She asked for help, too—"which I hate to do," she admits. She found volunteers to assist with her community work and began assigning more projects to the people she managed. The additional support enabled her to handle the commitments she already had (Delegation link).

As soon as Carol's work began to flow again, she made office organization a higher priority. A few hours spent clearing the physical clutter cleared her mind, as well, and relieved some stress. She realized that piles on her desk were signals that she was taking on—and holding onto—more than her share of work.

From the moment Carol looked at her situation from the Productivity Chain perspective, she felt empowered. "It explained so much," she says. It also gave her a sense of control because she had a clear plan of action. Within a couple of weeks of consciously focusing on her weak links, her outlook brightened, her output actually increased, and her overwhelm dissolved.

How the Productivity Chain Model Can Help You, Too

You can experience the same benefits that Carol did. The Productivity Chain is a life-changer, yet you need no special training or tools to apply it. In a very short time, Carol realized, learned, and mentally shifted a great deal. The Chain is so quickly transformative because it serves several much-needed, yet distinct functions at once. Each one helps you achieve the results you want.

The Productivity Chain is:

- **An instruction manual.** It explains what fosters productivity, what blocks it, and how you can leverage improvements in key links to become more effective. (See Chapter 2: *How the Productivity Chain Functions.*)
- **A mindset.** The Productivity Chain shifts you from frustrated and powerless to powerful, responsible, and action-oriented in every area of your life—all by changing your perspective. (See Chapter 3: *A Powerful Perspective.*)
- **An assessment tool.** The Chain helps you assess yourself and your situation, defining your problems in ways that lead to specific, practical, and effective solutions. (See Chapter 4: *Identify Solutions, The Productivity Chain Analysis.*)
- **A call to action.** Chain solutions always involve concrete action directed at particular links. The process is simple and applicable to any link and situation. (See Chapter 5: *Strengthen Your Weak Links.*)
- **A performance standard.** The "Power Chain" describes the benefits you receive when all your links are "strong enough." This standard can guide your self-improvement efforts, clarifying that you will achieve greater productivity, not perfection. (See Chapter 6: *The Power Chain.*)
- **A guiding framework.** The Productivity Chain provides the bigger picture into which all the productivity-related puzzle pieces fit, enabling you to filter through information more easily and spend your self-improvement money and time more wisely. (See Chapter 7: *A Guiding Framework.*)

1: A NEW PRODUCTIVITY MODEL

The remaining chapters in this section explore these functions in greater depth. This section also ends with a case study that brings the Productivity Chain to life.

While many examples of the Productivity Chain in action involve overcoming struggles, the Chain is not just a tool for crisis intervention. If you are already highly productive, the Chain can raise your game still further. It also enables you to maintain, not just attain, a high performance level. The more you apply it, the more it helps.

Over time, the Productivity Chain becomes a habit of thought and action. It is a powerful approach to work and life, as the next chapters reveal.

> The Productivity Chain enables you to **maintain**, not just attain, a high performance level.

2 How the Productivity Chain Functions

"Our strength grows out of our weakness."
—Ralph Waldo Emerson

The more you understand the twelve links and how their connections affect your Productivity Chain as a whole, the more successfully and easily you can leverage those links to boost your own performance.

This chapter addresses key points about the Chain and how people have benefited from applying that knowledge. They are:

- Your links vary in strength.
- Your links' strengths change.
- Your links interact.
- You can leverage the "Chain Reaction."

Your Links Vary in Strength

Some links in your Chain are more solid than others. No one has twelve links of equal strength, whether strong, medium, or weak. This imbalance has four important implications.

1. Strong links can compensate for weaker links.

Often, strong links can compensate for weaker ones—to a point.

Raymond's Story

Raymond, a director of operations for a 500-person company, had links of steel when it came to Task/Project Management, Resources (especially his high intelligence and amazing memory), and Drive. His CEO called him "a machine"—his highest praise—because Raymond would just crank out the results.

2: HOW THE PRODUCTIVITY CHAIN FUNCTIONS

He needed those strong links because Raymond's Boundary-setting link was relatively weak. His coworkers imposed on his giving nature frequently. He often did their work for them because he thought saying "no" might damage the relationships.

His family life (Health link) suffered because doing those favors took time away from them, but Raymond's stronger links lessened the impact—for now. Who knows, though, what he could achieve if he didn't spend so much time doing other people's tasks. Someday, if his Health (or another) link weakens enough, his strong links won't be able to compensate anymore.

> At some point, Raymond's strong links won't be able to compensate for his weak ones anymore.

2. Other people may not realize your weaknesses.

Others may have no idea that you struggle in certain areas, but that does not make those weak links any less troubling. "Even my brother does not know I'm chronically disorganized," says Ava, a private banker.

"He'll say, 'I thought you were very organized.' I don't know if I've portrayed that. Maybe it's because I'm so successful in my career. Maybe some of those other links of mine are so much stronger that I'm able to hide it. But Organization of Objects/Data is probably my weakest link. Weak, but improving."

3. Weak links put strain on other links.

Weak links are often the hidden reason a strong link does not operate to its potential.

Breyen's Story

Breyen was a commanding leader, the CEO of his design firm. He possessed a clear vision and the ability to get things done—when he did them. Despite his enthusiasm, his people never seemed to "get it." His Communication/Relationships link was weak. He did not convey his messages to others in ways that inspired them to embrace his goals and implement his plans.

He had to rely heavily on oversight and accountability (his Delegation link) to essentially force people to do their work. And he had to force himself to stay positive (his Drive link). His poor Communication/Relationships link strained these stronger links.

4. Very weak links can render strong links moot.

Here is the real danger of especially weak links: they can break, shattering your overall performance for days, weeks, or longer.

Becky's Story

Becky, an office manager, had effective task and project management systems, well-organized objects and data, and strong planning and communication skills. Sounds like someone who can really produce, right? Right—when she was healthy. Becky also experienced recurring major depression.

> One weak link can undermine the effects of other links—even your strong ones.

During an episode, which might last weeks or months, she lacked physical energy, drive, motivation, and focus. She brought her body to work but her mind did not fully engage. "When you're trying to work when you are depressed, it's like running a marathon in a swamp," she explains. "It's very, very difficult and frustrating." When depressed, her weak Health link snapped her Drive link and shut her down. It rendered her strong links moot.

Your Links' Strengths Change

Your particular combination of strengths and weaknesses varies over time and circumstances. By implementing the ideas in this book, for instance, you will make certain links stronger.

Many situations affect your Chain's strength—and its ability to transmit power. When you get a new job, for instance, your performance is not as strong as it will be once you learn the ropes—that is, until your Resources link, which includes job-specific knowledge and skills—improves.

Sometimes the change happens slowly. If your work conditions remain relentlessly grueling for an extended period of time, you may get burned out as your Drive link thins. By responding swiftly with needed respite, however, the damage is only temporary.

Betty's Story

The change in links can be dramatic. Betty, an executive director of a not-for-profit organization, helped her weakest link become her strongest. She used to set unrealistically high goals for herself and

2: HOW THE PRODUCTIVITY CHAIN FUNCTIONS

then felt like a failure when she couldn't achieve them. She wanted to make thirty phone calls a week to development prospects, for example, but rarely picked up the phone.

To strengthen her Goal-setting/Prioritization link, she first acknowledged that development was just one of her many responsibilities. She then made her development goal more achievable: fifteen prospect calls a week.

> It took me a while to accept the limits on what I can do, but now it's really paying off. I feel like I'm in control.
> Betty, executive director

Forced to prioritize her calls, she selected only the most promising potential donors. By focusing on quality, not quantity, she raised more funds in less time. "It took me a while to accept the limits on what I can do, but now it's really paying off," Betty reports. "I feel like I'm in control." That year, she set a personal record for sponsor contributions.

The purpose of this book is to empower you to strengthen your weak links and transform your productivity, as Betty did.

Your Links Interact

The links in your Productivity Chain influence each other in complex ways. Certain links are themselves two or more highly-related yet distinct factors, such as Communication and Relationships. The reason for grouping them is sheer manageability. The goal of the model is simplicity without over simplification.

One-to-one interactions

Even for links that seem straightforward, such as Boundary-setting, the connections to other links can be so intricate that it is difficult to distinguish where one link ends and another begins. You set boundaries by communicating (Communication/Relationships link), for example. You also protect your time (Planning link) by setting boundaries.

You might think of the Chain as fused together rather than interlocking, so tight are the bonds. The closer the connection, the more quickly you experience the effects when one link changes. Each chapter of Section II: *The Twelve Links* includes a chart indicating how that chapter's link interacts with every other link.

THE PRODUCTIVITY CHAIN

Multiple-links interactions
Sometimes multiple links interact at once. You can see this phenomenon in the common scenario of talking with an employee about her job performance.

Frank's Story
Frank, CEO of a commercial printing firm, felt frustrated by his head of administration, Julia. She was a wonderful person who had been with him a long time. She generally did a good job. She set a bad example with her long lunches, however, and her articles for the company newsletter were poorly written and sometimes inaccurate. Frank wanted to set limits around Julia's performance and clarify his expectations and standards (Boundary-setting link).

He also wanted to maintain a positive rapport with Julia because he liked her and they worked closely together. He needed his message to be positive, respectful, direct, and clear (Communication/Relationships link). Her work enabled him to do his (Delegation link), after all, and achieve the results he wanted (Goal-setting/Prioritization link).

Unfortunately, based on past experience, Frank expected Julia to get defensive and then give him the cold shoulder for a few days after he addressed her behavior. He avoided conflict when possible, which led him to approach this conversation with reluctance (Drive link).

In fact, when Frank finally talked with Julia, he softened his message so much that his clear expectations became vague suggestions. He did not even mention a follow-up appointment to assess progress. The blurrier his supervision, the less potential for conflict. He really did like Julia, he told himself, rationalizing, and did not want to lose her. (He had no reason to fear she might quit).

What happened? One ten-minute conversation, with five links in play, resulted in one weak Drive link undermining the others—reducing Frank's effectiveness.

You Can Leverage the "Chain Reaction"
Improving one link sparks change in other areas. As Rosa, an ad executive who improved her Task/Project Management link, says, "It gives you a whole new perspective on the possible. Once you do

2: HOW THE PRODUCTIVITY CHAIN FUNCTIONS

something that you didn't think you could do, you start to become confident that you can do more."

Strengthening one link has a multiplicative, even exponential, effect on your overall productivity. Even if you don't directly address other links, they feel the benefit. I call this impact the Chain Reaction. It occurs because your whole Chain is greater than the sum of its parts.

> Strengthening one link has a multiplicative, even exponential, effect on your overall productivity.

When your weakest link becomes strong enough not to impair your other links, you experience the Power Chain, a special kind Chain Reaction described in Chapter 6.

Max's Story

Max experienced the Chain Reaction. His assessment revealed that this construction firm executive had a relatively weak Boundary-setting link; he found it difficult to stand up for himself. His office was also quite disorganized; he had no "homes" for items and often had to hunt for files. He had always struggled with "stuff."

Since reinforcing the Organization of Objects/Data link produces visible results relatively quickly, we started there. Over the course of several hours, we transformed his workspace and established systems so Max could maintain the new order.

When we met again a couple weeks later, Max mentioned that he had begun setting limits with some coworkers who routinely asked him to look up information and records that they themselves should find. I asked Max what prompted this new, more assertive behavior.

"I feel better about myself after getting my office organized," he replied. "They can see I've changed. I'm not going to keep doing other people's work." Even though we hadn't yet begun addressing boundary-setting, strengthening one link naturally benefitted another.

As he grew more assertive, speaking up about his ideas and requesting what he needed, Max's overall productivity stayed high. Best of all, his stress level and enjoyment of his work improved.

3 A Powerful Perspective

"My wife is threatening to leave and my kids barely talk to me."
  —*John, CEO of a conglomerate*
"I want to take my work to a higher level. I think I could be even more effective."
  —*Peggy, bank branch manager*

If you relate to these comments, you are part of a large and growing group of people—the frustrated professional. You have a problem: you are not as productive as you would like to be. The problem may be lifelong, or at least since middle school. It may be new, since your second child's birth, for instance.

The situation might be dire. You could lose your job if you do not change your ways, for example. Or it might be more aspirational: You want an edge over the competition or more time with your family. Whatever the specifics, you have a problem (see box) or opportunity and you want it solved.

The Problem with "Problem"

The word "problem" gets an undeserved bad rap these days. Some people prefer to use "issues" or "challenges," as if changing the word changes the reality that some situations need to be addressed and improved. Now those replacement words have gained the same negative connotation as "problem."

In fact, the word "problem" is actually neutral and descriptive. It means a confusing or complicated subject or a question needing a solution.[3] Nothing bad about that. I prefer to use "problem" because "solution" is built into its definition.

3: A POWERFUL PERSPECTIVE

The Symptoms

You probably first become aware of your problem by noticing its symptoms. As you read the common indicators below, which hit home? What other symptoms do you experience?

TAKE ACTION
Identify the symptoms you notice at work and home.

- You regularly work longer hours than you would like.
- You receive 150 emails or more each day.
- Your follow-through has declined—things fall through the cracks too often.
- You sense you are not achieving as much as you could or functioning as efficiently as you could.
- Your mind feels stuffed with all your to-do's.
- You frequently shift your systems, processes, goals, or apps.
- You experience sleep troubles, either finding it difficult to fall asleep or waking up early with your mind racing about work.
- You sometimes feel overwhelmed or on the brink of it.
- You find yourself moving into avoidance mode, procrastinating on important tasks.
- You get sick more often or your personal relationships have become tense.

Robert, an executive for a military defense contractor, sought help because he started experiencing some of these symptoms, as well as moments of paralysis that were quite out of character. "There were a few days when I would walk in my office, sit down at my desk, and not know what to do," he says.

"There was just too much. And it all had to be done right now. I'd look at it and think, 'I can't do this.' Just complete frustration. The voice mail is flashing, there're ten text messages, and I'd sit there thinking, 'What do I do?'"

Typical Problem Labeling

At some point, your symptoms became undeniable. You might have had one of those days that Robert described. Maybe there was a crisis or it dawned on you gradually. Maybe you just compared

THE PRODUCTIVITY CHAIN

yourself to someone else. That's what Dez, a top-ten loan officer, did. He noticed that the bank's number one performer not only produced more, but seemed to have a more fulfilling personal life, too. That's when Dez realized what he himself lacked.

When that awareness arose in you, you knew you had a productivity problem. You probably didn't spend a lot of time analyzing it, identifying its roots and effects, pinpointing the possible solutions, and mapping out a plan to implement them. You were too busy dealing with those symptoms.

You probably did give your problem a name—a label—to describe it, though. Your label might have been vague and general, ("I'm disorganized") or specific ("I need to improve my follow-up"). Whether you knew it or not, that label instantly defined your problem and therefore its solution. As you may have discovered, when the label is wrong, the cure usually is, too.

New Labels, New Solutions

To understand the importance of problem definitions—of labels—imagine this symptom: you don't spend enough time on critical projects. You complete them late or keep re-setting the deadlines.

Your productivity problem seems obvious: you don't have enough time. It's a problem you probably hear people complain about often.

> *There are times when the greatest change needed is a change of my viewpoint.*
> —Denis Diderot

But what if you change your "diagnosis?" What if you shift your view? Instead of blaming time, you examine your Productivity Chain and identify your weak links—specific deficiencies in the way you function at work. You analyze which tangible skills, knowledge, and abilities may be under-developed, missing, or not applied. What happens? Immediately, strategic and tactical solutions occur to you.

To test yourself, read these two problem definitions out loud:

A. "I just don't have enough time to do it all."

B. "I'm not good at delegating. I do so much of what others could do that I don't get to my most important work."

How did you feel as you said each statement? Which explanation did you prefer?

3: A POWERFUL PERSPECTIVE

The Productivity Chain Difference
You may have noticed these key differences between the two problem definitions you just read:

- **Power:** There is more power in statement B. You *can* actually improve your delegation. It is a skill, not rocket science or an inherited trait. You have no power, however, to create more time. (To make a day last forty hours instead of twenty-four, for instance, you would have to slow the earth's rotation.)

- **Responsibility:** Statement A is a complaint and excuse. It implies that time, and not you, is responsible for your unmet goals. With statement B, however, you *own* your productivity problem and, therefore, its solution. Taking responsibility enables response-ability.

- **Action-ability:** Problem definition B automatically suggests a clear, concrete, and achievable solution—take action to improve your delegation skills. Definition A, on the other hand, leaves you stuck once again because you cannot change time.

Statement B exemplifies defining your problem from the Productivity Chain perspective. You can replace "delegating" with "decision-making," "planning," "prioritizing," and so on. Whatever your weak link, the Chain enables you to define a more manageable and solve-able problem.

Powerful Reframing
When you put your old problems into the new frame of the Productivity Chain, you view them differently and find new remedies. This shift in perspective is called "reframing."

So many productivity problems persist because we frame them in unhelpful ways. As a result, we waste time pursuing the wrong solutions or we get paralyzed, taking no action to improve our situations. Worst of all, we may come to believe that there is something wrong with us, when really our viewpoint is the culprit.

Over the years of practice and research, I have collected the unhelpful problem definitions common among my clients and others. These perspectives sometimes harden into beliefs that I call "Productivity Myths." Section III examines twelve in detail, including the ever-popular "I need more time" and "I need to get more organized" fictions (Chapters 22 and 24 respectively).

When you reframe your personal myths in terms of the Productivity Chain, you can approach your work with the energy generated by power, responsibility, and action.

> **TAKE ACTION**
> See Section III: *Productivity Myths* to learn how the Productivity Chain topples illusions about what gets in the way of optimal productivity.

That's what Bill, the founder of a start-up, found. "The Productivity Chain concept changed the way we solve problems around here," he explains. "We're more likely to pause before we decide what the depths of any problem are."

Work's "Victim" No More

The Productivity Chain perspective changes the way you think—and talk—about yourself and your work. It releases you from feeling you are at the mercy of your job—reacting to emails, putting out fires, pulled in all directions. Instead, you realize that the power to improve your situation resides within you.

Since a Productivity Chain problem always contains its solution, the actions that will improve your output and effectiveness become clear: flex or strengthen the relevant links. (See Chapter 5: *Strengthen Your Weak Links* for specifics.)

If you decide ***not*** to apply those links, that conscious decision is still an act of personal power or agency. Even if you continue to blame time, Fate, or others, you recognize that this, too, is a choice. Deep down, you know you—not they—are responsible for yourself.

Few people consciously want to feel like a victim of Time—or anything else, for that matter. On a deeper level, though, victimhood frees them from responsibility for difficult decisions. Accepting the Productivity Chain premise means you can no longer say you did not do something because you "had no time," the "deadline passed you by," or—as they say in the military—the plan was "overcome by events."

In this model, life doesn't "happen" to you. Instead, you take full responsibility for your actions or inaction. You did not do the task because you went to your son's soccer game or you worked on

3: A POWERFUL PERSPECTIVE

something else instead, for instance. You made a decision—and possibly the right one. If you forgot a task, your "decision" was to be vague about your commitments. Your mistakes—and successes—belong to you.

This strong sense of responsibility reflects a return of your personal power and control, which is itself productivity-enhancing. (See Chapter 6: *The Power Chain* for more about the role of power in productivity.)

> This strong sense of responsibility reflects a return of your personal power and control, which is in itself productivity-enhancing.

Feeling out-of-control deflates performance and leads to avoidance. Research has shown that lack of autonomy correlates with lower productivity and fulfillment at work.[4] The Productivity Chain restores your autonomy, control, and—ultimately—your satisfaction.

That said, you may actually have too much on your plate. Some employers demand more output from fewer people all the time, chasing the next quarter's profit statement. Sometimes technology bridges the gaps, but often it can't. If you are part of the gig economy, you juggle multiple jobs to make ends meet. You may be self-employed, forced to wear many hats each day. In the 21st Century, we live and work within an economic system that requires ever more hustling with less stability and fewer (and sometimes no) traditional benefits. The problem is the system and the solution depends on people-driven systemic change.

In the meantime, the Productivity Chain enables you to wield the power you do have. If you determine that you operate as productively as possible and the problem is actually systemic, that definition points you towards specific actions, too, such as adjusting expectations with your supervisor (or yourself), collective bargaining, and so on. These actions fall into the Communication/Relationships link.

When the demands remain unrealistic, being productive may mean focusing on what matters most, clarifying expectations about what will get done later or not at all, and learning to live with the resulting discomfort in ways that allow you to be present mentally and emotionally for life outside of work. The Productivity Chain perspective can help with all of that, too.

4 Identify Solutions
The Productivity Chain Analysis

"We can't solve problems by using the same kind of thinking we used when we created them."
—Albert Einstein

Defining productivity problems in specific, skills-oriented ways leads to targeted, practical solutions. That is the power of the Productivity Chain perspective.

Tips, tricks, tools, systems, and products can improve your productivity. This book offers many. You make the greatest, most efficient gains, however, when you know **which** tips, tricks, tools, systems, and products best meet your needs. That is where the Productivity Chain Analysis comes in. Analyzing your Chain enables you to identify the best solutions for your productivity problems, so you can take effective action.

The Productivity Chain Analysis is simple: Identify which links need to be made stronger. (See the box on the next page.) Since each link represents a set of knowledge, skills, and abilities, your solution is to take concrete action to develop those areas.

Three Types of Productivity Chain Analysis

You can use your Chain to assess your productivity in three ways:

A. **Self-Assessment:** The self-assessment is a broad, thorough review of your current experience and history to identify your strong and weak links. This approach can enhance your overall performance. (I have every client complete one to supplement the evaluation I make.)

B. **Situation Analysis:** This analysis focuses more narrowly on a single productivity symptom to pinpoint its root causes. When

4: IDENTIFY SOLUTIONS (THE PC ANALYSIS)

> **Why Focus on Strengths and Weaknesses?**
>
> Some people think you should develop only your strengths and ignore your flaws. RJ, a management consultant, summarizes this view, saying "You don't want a bunch of 'strong weaknesses.' Focus on your strengths, and surround yourself with people who can compensate for your weaknesses." It makes sense—if your weaker links are fairly sturdy and if you're surrounded by competent people who can help.
>
> Most people are not that fortunate. If one of your links has a hidden hairline fracture, you're in trouble. Eventually, your productivity will crack under stress—and it may take down others' productivity, too. (See Myth Chapter 29: *Others Can Make Up for What I Lack*.)
>
> > Take a balanced approach to your Productivity Chain. Target weaknesses to avoid failure. Target strengths to create success.
>
> As Malena, an accountant, puts it, "If the weak links are not addressed, the best you're going to end up with is organized chaos. You may have seasons where things are going well, but sooner or later, they're going to get you. You just don't know when and to what extent."
>
> In fact, there's no empirical evidence that focusing solely on strengths is effective. It might even be detrimental, since over-developed strengths can become weaknesses themselves.[5] Can you imagine an Olympic runner building up her already-strong quadriceps while ignoring her weak hamstrings? It does not make sense.
>
> Taking a balanced look at your Productivity Chain's strengths and weaknesses ensures that all your links meet a basic threshold of effectiveness. Address your weaknesses to avoid failure. You don't want your Achilles heel to take you out of the race. Then focus on your strengths to create success and win the race.

you address every link in the Chain that contributes to the situation, you solve it completely.

C. **Instant Reframe:** This approach can be done in a moment. Renaming and reframing a problem from the Chain perspective instantly increases your sense of power and control and directs you towards positive action. Down the road, you can use a Situation Analysis to resolve the matter completely.

THE PRODUCTIVITY CHAIN

Each type of Productivity Chain Analysis has value. The Self-Assessment is best for guiding general self-improvement efforts, particularly when your circumstances are stable. The Situation Analysis works well when you feel overwhelmed, nearing crisis, or concerned about a single matter. You can use the Instant Reframe to make adjustments if your high level of performance starts to slide, or to ease yourself into using the Chain for the first time.

The remainder of this chapter describes in more detail how to use these three methods of Productivity Chain Analysis.

A. Self-Assessment

You may already know your productivity strengths and weaknesses on some level—or think that you do. At our first appointment, Teri, the CEO of a recruiting firm, calmly said, "I never plan. I like to take life as it comes." Sure enough, the more we talked, the clearer it became that Planning *was* her weakest link. It affected her deeply. Her productivity solution would lie in a handful of practical techniques that helped her think ahead and get into her calendar—i.e., to strengthen her Planning link.

Other times, however, you may not realize what gets in your way. Some clients assess themselves as good managers, for instance. The reviews from their teams, however, say otherwise. We all have blind spots—we don't know what we don't know. That's why it helps to assess yourself by asking specific questions about your thoughts and behaviors, not your general opinions of yourself.

Performing a Self-Assessment

You can identify your strong and weak links through a Self-Assessment in a number of ways:

- Take the full Productivity Chain Self-Assessment (or the quick quiz) at *www.CaseyMooreInc.com* and receive an instant and detailed report.
- Read about the links in Section II: *The Twelve Links* and the topics they encompass in Appendix C: *Productivity-Related Terms*. The better you understand each link, the more accurately you can assess your own.

4: IDENTIFY SOLUTIONS (THE PC ANALYSIS)

- Ask those who work with you to give you feedback about what they observe and experience.
- Do the exercises and take the actions in this book with someone whose feedback you trust.

TAKE ACTION
Take the Productivity Chain Self-Assessment or the quiz at *CaseyMooreInc.com*.

Kraygin's Story

Once you know which link(s) to improve, you can take action. That's what Kraygin, a chief financial officer, did. His Productivity Chain Self-Assessment revealed that he needed to improve his Reinvention link in order to handle change and surprises more effectively.

Kraygin thrived on routine and structure. When unforeseen events upset his plans, however, he lost focus. He wasted time searching for someone or something to blame, which derailed his day even further. As a result, he felt stressed out and worked late and most weekends.

To strengthen his Reinvention link, Kraygin committed to view change as opportunity, rather than failure. He also practiced making more flexible plans, leaving room for what I call "the predictably unpredictable." When urgent situations arose, he had enough cushion in his calendar and his mind to absorb them.

Sometimes Kraygin still became anxious when life threw him a curve ball. Compared to how he reacted before, however, the improvement was great. It was certainly enough to keep that one weakness from nullifying his strengths. Eventually, it shaved time from his work week and improved his relationship with his coworkers.

Peggy's Story

Peggy, a bank branch manager, thought she needed a clone of herself to help handle her many commitments, both professional and personal. Her Self-Assessment identified Delegation and Health (lack of sleep) as her weak links. The results were no surprise, but they were validating.

She took immediate action—going to bed earlier and handing off more tasks and projects to others, including her children. With better sleep, Peggy grew more confident and optimistic. She initially felt nervous about entrusting her work to others and wanted to take it all back when she discovered errors. Still, she kept delegating. She realized the payoffs—more manageable days—outweighed the risks. And they gave others the chance to grow.

B. Situation Analysis

Sometimes a symptom reflects the interactions of many links in a single situation. You can solve the underlying problems at root level by focusing on whether—and how—each link contributes to that one difficulty. Email overload, a common productivity quagmire, benefits from such a Situation Analysis, as Amanda's experience demonstrates.

Amanda's Story

Amanda, a human resources director, was drowning in her email. The alerts interrupted her throughout the day and she found them difficult to resist. Others admired how quickly Amanda responded to their messages, thinking she was "on top of it." Meanwhile, she often completed key projects late because they required a concentration she lacked. Her focus was too fragmented.

Just opening her email app made Amanda feel anxious and "overwhelmed." It seemed to reflect her own cluttered mind. She had over 7,000 messages in her in-box, not counting those filed haphazardly in various folders. Most were relics of completed communications, but many still required action. Once an email moved out of view on her computer screen, however, it usually slipped out of mind, too.

If Amanda lived in an alternate universe where she had unlimited time and energy, she could handle each email completely when it arrived and still complete her other work. In this world, she had to adopt new email habits to stay afloat.

Each new habit strengthened a particular weakness in her Productivity Chain. Combined, these new practices helped her dramatically reduce the number of emails she received. At the same time, they enabled her to increase her speed and effectiveness in responding to the emails she did get.

4: IDENTIFY SOLUTIONS (THE PC ANALYSIS)

The Productivity Chain Cure for Email Overload
Here is how Amanda became the master of her email domain:

Getting Started
- She committed to changing her approach towards email, determined to control it rather than the other way around. Instead of seeing it as an unexpected flood that derailed her day, she accepted it as a predictable source of unpredictable work. **Drive and Reinvention**
- She took a software class to learn practical tips for managing emails. **Resources**

Limiting Emails
- She set limits with technology by turning off the alerts and checking email when *she* wanted, which was usually every fifteen to thirty minutes. **Boundary-setting**
- She began forwarding emails to the appropriate person to handle certain questions she received, whereas in the past she would have just answered them herself. She copied the senders so they would contact the right person next time. **Delegation**
- She started making more phone calls, finding she could resolve some matters—especially intricate or sensitive ones—faster that way. **Communication/ Relationships**
- She met with those who frequently copied her on emails to discuss which situations actually merited her attention. Some "cc'd" Amanda as leverage to force others to act or to cover their own actions or inaction. Others simply wanted to keep her in the loop. **Communication/ Relationships and Delegation**

  She coached them on more effective ways to manage their people and communicate with her, so they could stop unnecessarily copying her on messages.

THE PRODUCTIVITY CHAIN

Handling Emails

- She set a goal to have twenty or fewer emails in her in-box at any time. When they piled up, she made processing them a priority. — **Goal-setting/Prioritization**

- She ruthlessly decided how to handle emails when they arrived, filing as few and deleting as many as she could. She responded immediately and completely if the response took just a minute or two. — **Decision-making**

- She flagged emails that still required her attention, including those she sent to others asking questions, so she could see all outstanding matters in one folder/view. She reviewed these items every morning to see which she needed to follow up on that day. — **Task/Project Management**

- She dragged emails that would take thirty minutes or more to complete onto her calendar, scheduling time to address them. — **Planning**

- She and her direct-reports agreed on an email shorthand so she could type directives at the beginning of email subject lines, saving keystrokes and time. Their code included RI (Resolve Issue), FYI (For Your Information), and SA (Schedule Appointment). — **Communication/Relationships and Delegation**

- She set up a simpler email filing system to hold the messages she wanted to save for future reference. Having few folders made searches quicker and moving "completed" emails from her in-box easier. — **Organization of Objects/Data**

- She sometimes timed herself as she wrote emails. It drove her to be as brief, fast, and accurate as possible. It made email a game. — **Drive**

- She began getting more rest. The more alert she was, the faster and better she handled her emails. — **Health**

4: IDENTIFY SOLUTIONS (THE PC ANALYSIS)

Amanda's experience shows why so many efforts to improve performance fail—they only address one part of the picture. Many people think, "I have too many emails. I need to use Outlook or Gmail better." But had Amanda only focused on software solutions, her success would have been limited. She still would have had too many emails to handle.

In the end, all twelve links played a part in Amanda's problem and its solution. No wonder email derails so many people's productivity! The Situation Analysis solved Amanda's email problem. (It might solve yours, too.)

C. Instant Reframe

Sometimes you just need a new way to view a problem to break yourself out of a rut. Renaming your problem as a weak link in your Productivity Chain immediately suggests practical steps you can take to improve your productivity. Just choose the link most obviously related to your symptom and take one positive action to strengthen it.

This on-the-spot Productivity Chain gut-check replaces your existing unappealing or ineffective problem/solution analysis with a more positive and actionable one. It may not be the only possible or "correct" solution, but it will increase your sense of power and responsibility.

Here are two examples of the Instant Reframe in action. You can see one for each link in the Chain in Appendix B: *Instant Reframe Examples*.

Example 1

The Symptom
You have lost interest in work and are just going through the motions.

Conventional Analysis
Problem: Your work isn't challenging anymore and the environment is not stimulating enough.
Solution: Find a new job.

> **TAKE ACTION**
> See Appendix B for Instant Reframe examples for all twelve links.

Productivity Chain Instant Reframe

Reframed Problem: You have become less engaged and have lost your motivation. (Your Drive link is weak.)

Instant Action: Identify one way to improve your own performance today (acting engaged increases engagement) or take on a new, challenging, growth-inducing responsibility.

Example 2

The Symptom

Reports take a long time to produce. You feel like you reinvent the wheel every time.

Conventional Analysis

Problem: The company requires too many reports and they are too complicated.

Solution: Work more hours if necessary to complete them.

Productivity Chain Instant Reframe

Reframed Problem: You are not using the company's custom software to its full potential to produce these reports. (Your Resources link is weak.)

Instant Action: Sign up for your company's regular software training class. In the meantime, use its Help feature or ask a proficient coworker for tips to finish today's report a little quicker.

Reframing your problem in terms of the links of the Productivity Chain in this quick and simple way may inspire you to do a more comprehensive analysis later on. In the meantime, it gets you moving in a positive direction.

That's because each Productivity Chain Analysis puts the focus on you, not factors outside yourself. It therefore directs your power where it can have an immediate effect.

5 Strengthen Your Weak Links

"It's all about taking action—one baby step at a time."
—Irene, director of quality assurance

Once you understand the true nature of your productivity difficulties, the solution to address what is within your control is simple and always the same: apply or strengthen the links in your Productivity Chain. When you shore up your weak links, they do not undermine your overall effectiveness. This chapter tells you how.

Make Your Weak Links Just "Strong Enough"

Your weaker links do not need to become as strong as all the others. They just need to be strong enough so that they don't destabilize your strengths—and so that they don't crack under pressure, rupturing your entire Chain.

Inez' Story

Inez, a team leader, found that her weakest link decreased her entire department's productivity. She was supremely organized (a solid Organization of Objects/Data link). Her Communication/Relationships link was strong, too. Her staff liked her and wanted to help her succeed. Her conversations were clear, direct, and full of active listening.

Because she had a weak Decision-making link, though, Inez' communication involved a lot of saying, "We need to push back the deadline by two weeks." Her indecision caused such delays in projects that she constantly hurtled from one deadline-driven crisis to another, dragging her team down with her.

THE PRODUCTIVITY CHAIN

> You can only be as productive as your weakest link allows.

Through coaching, Inez learned to put her decisions in perspective, labeling them either "mountains," "mole hills," or "ant hills." These categories helped her limit how much time she spent on a given decision: no more than two minutes for ant hills, two days for mole hills, and more for mountains (which were rare).

Her decisions were not always perfect, but they were better than paralysis. Her Decision-making link became strong enough so that everyone else could get on with their work, too.

Brody's Story

Here's how Brody, a vice president of sales who used to have a weak Task/Project Management link, explains the powerful effect of small improvements in his weak area: "I am sort of a generalist, big-picture-type person. The details I know I'm not going to be perfect with, so I settle for being better than I was."

While working with me, Brody developed a number of new habits that strengthened his skills. Together, those habits formed a system unique to him. "My new Task Management system has helped me so much," he says. "It gave me confidence that even though that wasn't my strength, it's not going to be my downfall, either. I can focus on what I do best, which is getting to meetings, making the presentations, having the relationships. And I'm not going to let 'Did you call so-and-so back quickly enough' be the reason that I don't get the business."

Learn from Your Strong Links

Success breeds success. One way to strengthen your weak links is by learning from your strong links. Identify what makes them strong, then translate that to your weaker links.

Alex's Story

Alex ran the service department for a car dealership and his Communication/Relationships link was his strongest. He liked taking his customers' calls and enjoyed talking with them at the counter.

His Planning and Drive links, meanwhile, were weak. His

5: STRENGTHEN YOUR WEAK LINKS

schedule had no structure (Planning link). He liked being interrupted by people, especially when he had to do the administrative part of his job, which he disliked (Drive link). He often had to work late to complete his customers' orders and reports as a result.

Alex reflected on his Communication/Relationships link and realized ***why*** it was so strong: He loved people. He found almost everyone interesting. He liked learning about them and helping them in any way he could. Alex used this information to improve his weak links.

He decided to see his "paperwork" as a way to care for his customers—a subtle, yet powerful, perspective shift that strengthened his Drive link. He became more motivated, especially when he visualized the customer he was helping.

TAKE ACTION
Write down the reasons your three strongest links are so strong. How can that information help you strengthen your three weakest links?

Alex also began to schedule an "appointment" with a particular customer's file to do that work—a simple improvement to his Planning link. Together, these small, practical changes transformed his productivity on the administrative side of his job.

Take Concrete Actions

There are many ways to strengthen the links in your Productivity Chain. They usually involve educating yourself and forming new habits. If, for example, you need to improve your communication (Communication/Relationships link), you can:

- Read Chapter 9: *Communication/Relationships*.
- Read other books and articles on how to communicate effectively. (See Appendix D: *Productivity-Related Resources* for ideas.)
- Watch TED talks or other videos on listening and speaking.
- Attend workshops on communication.
- Interview good communicators and ask their advice.
- Observe people who communicate well and analyze what works.
- Observe people who communicate poorly to learn from their

mistakes.
- Hire a coach to work with you one-to-one.
- Practice participating in difficult or sensitive conversations by role-playing with a friend.
- Video yourself listening and speaking so you can hear and/or see how you come across to others (with their permission).
- Try out new ways of interacting with others, always reflecting on what works and what doesn't.

The list goes on. An abundance of learning opportunities flood in once you specify your weak link. The same applies for any link in the Chain.

6 The Power Chain

"The last few years have been amazing. Numbers-wise, my productivity has never been better. And I've got a great family life, too. Life's not perfect, but what I've got feels solid. I'm not worried the way I used to be."
 —Dustin, publisher

When the weakest link in your Productivity Chain is strong enough to coordinate with the other links, rather than undermine them, you experience a special kind of the Chain Reaction described in Chapter 2: *How the Productivity Chain Functions*.

You receive the productivity benefits that each link offers, of course. But when those links cooperate, your whole Chain becomes far stronger than the sum of its parts. It takes your performance to a higher—and deeper—level. This is the Power Chain. Its gifts extend into every facet of your life, both professional and personal.

Power Flows through "Strong Enough" Links

The Power Chain does not require supernatural strength in all your links. In fact, they don't have to be especially strong—just "strong enough." Your productivity power flows when no link in your Chain is so weak that it debilitates the others.

Think of holiday lights. If all the bulbs on a string are big and bright except one, the electricity will not flow through that dud to the next bulbs, no matter how sound they are. When the string is a closed circuit (like your Productivity Chain), **all** its lights shut down. When that weak bulb is strong enough to conduct just a little charge, however, the power flowing through it lights up the night.

THE PRODUCTIVITY CHAIN

> You don't need every link to be extremely strong. You just can't have **any** link be extremely weak.

Once you strengthen your weakest link or links sufficiently, the Power Chain effect begins. You achieve it through action—not genetics. (See Productivity Myth Chapter 28: *I Am Not Naturally Productive* for details.)

You Control the Flow

You have probably experienced the Power Chain effect already, although you didn't call it that. You just knew you performed at a high level and enjoyed it. You were in a state of flow. With the insight you gain through the Productivity Chain model, you can better understand exactly how the Power Chain occurs—and how you can revive it when it starts to wane.

The Power Chain effect can't last forever—your links and life are too dynamic for that. While temporarily-weakened links might cause your power connection to waver occasionally, you will enjoy the Power Chain so much that you find yourself adjusting quickly to regain that flow.

Those adjustments enable you to maintain a Power Chain for weeks, months, even years, at a time—as Dustin's statement at the beginning of this chapter reveals. It creates a "Golden Age" of productivity for you.

Power Chain Benefits

The Power Chain makes your work more fulfilling and enjoyable. You may not have realized you lacked a certain level of productivity, clarity, power, and peace until your Power Chain restores it to you. It's a gift you want to share with others, to help them, too.

The Power Chain benefits are not theoretical. They are the experience of my clients and others. Will you enjoy these gifts every minute of every day? No. You can, however, achieve them more frequently and with less effort than you do now. They are:

1. Sustainably High Productivity

The Power Chain yields consistently and sustainably high performance because all your links work in harmony—from setting

6: THE POWER CHAIN

Productivity Benefits of the Power Chain

- You consistently produce at high levels.
- You develop clear goals and achieve them on time and on budget.
- You manage interruptions and new information calmly and appropriately; you are not thrown off when your plans get disrupted.
- You develop and sharpen the skills, knowledge, and abilities required by your profession.
- You leave your work at work, using your personal time to engage in pursuits that refresh you.
- Your stress level energizes you without pushing you over the edge into avoidance or errors.
- You have clear systems to monitor and manage your workload, allowing progress with clarity.
- You spend appropriate time on decision-making, using the best information at hand.

- You respect yourself and earn respect from others, being neither a pushover nor a naysayer.
- You end your days with a sense of accomplishment and value.
- You plan your work and protect your time so you experience fewer crises and distractions.
- You are focused and highly motivated, fueled by your internal drive to succeed.
- You spend most of your time on important tasks, letting go of the trivial.
- You train, respect, and rely on others to do their jobs so you can focus on your high-value activities.
- You work efficiently, readily accessing tools and information as you need them.
- You develop deeper relationships with others, including clients and coworkers, as you become more "present" with them.

relevant, results-driven goals (Goal-setting/Prioritization link); to creating plans to achieve the goals and arranging adequate time to do the work (Planning link); to managing interruptions so you can carry out the plans (Boundary-setting link). See the box above for a list of some productivity benefits.

2. Greater Clarity

The Power Chain generates clarity. Clarity means you know what you need to do and when to do it. You are clear about what matters most and least. You know your own strengths, weaknesses, needs, and resources.

With a Power Chain, you use systems and strategies that free your mind of clutter so you can respond creatively in the moment to any situation. It helps you be present and engaged. A clear mind also allows you to fall—and stay—asleep more easily (Health link).

3. Enhanced Personal Power

"Power" is, essentially, the capacity to act, to do, to control.[6] Your "personal power" is your control over **yourself**—your perceptions, opinions, decisions, actions, and so on. It has a relatively small sphere of influence but its effects can be enormous.

> A hidden cause of productivity problems is stifled, misdirected, or forfeited personal power.

When you apply your power to strengthen your weak links, you make a Power Chain, which, in turn, becomes a conduit for your power. It enhances your power by letting it flow freely through all your links.

One hidden, yet significant, cause of many people's productivity problems is stifled, misdirected, or forfeited personal power.

- **Stifled:** When you routinely ignore, deny, or repress who you are, you leave no room for your personal power to flow. You arrived on this planet with a life force, gifts, and intrinsic value as a human being. It takes a lot of (wasted) energy to keep a lid on all that.

- **Misdirected:** When you use your personal power to try to control or change other people, you waste it. Those efforts inevitably fail. Meanwhile, you starve parts of yourself that need that energy and attention.

- **Forfeited:** When you give your power away, you lose control of your life. You might forfeit your power to others (e.g., "I can't say no" or "I must accept every meeting request"), to technology (e.g., "I hear a ring, so I must answer"), or to Fate (e.g., "I have to endure, rather than help shape, events"). The list goes on.

6: THE POWER CHAIN

These misuses of personal power increase your stress, decrease your productivity, create resentments, and diminish your quality of life.

Working with your Power Chain, on the other hand, means not squandering your energy on matters, activities, and people beyond your control. It means being focused, taking full responsibility for your life and work. This book shows you many practical ways to do just that.

4. More Peace of Mind

The Power Chain allows you to perform your work peacefully, without turmoil about the process. Your work flows freely like a river, avoiding the dams of clutter, confusion, and denial. Peace occurs for many reasons.

- You have peace of mind because you complete your most important work first—and know exactly what is still undone.
- You have peace of mind because you avoid procrastination and perfectionism.
- You have peace of mind because you maintain perspective; you work in ways that fit your values and beliefs.
- You have peace of mind because you apply your personal power on yourself—where it can actually have a positive effect.

5. Increased Ability to Help Others

The Power Chain enables you to help others overcome their productivity problems, as you overcame—and continue to overcome—yours.

- **It increases your awareness**. Having moved out of the problem and into the solution in your own life, you have perspective to notice the productivity struggles of others.
- **It increases your insight.** Rather than label a direct-report "disorganized" because he seems scattered and his desk is a bit cluttered, for example, you consider all twelve links in his Productivity Chain to identify how you might be helpful to him.
- **It increases your credibility.** When you share with him what really improves performance, your words carry more weight

THE PRODUCTIVITY CHAIN

because they come from personal experience, rather than theory.

- **It increases your effectiveness.** Guiding him through a Productivity Chain Analysis, you can help him address root causes, not just symptoms. These causes point him towards practical solutions.

  Together, you may determine, for example, that his filing has become backed-up because he spends his time helping his fellow employees instead of applying his well-developed Organization of Objects/Data link's skills.

  Encouraging him to develop his Goal-setting/Prioritization and Boundary-setting links so he could balance his helping with doing his own work would restore his productivity much faster than sending him to a class on "getting organized" or generic "time management."

- **It increases your compassion.** You may one day have a colleague whose productivity struggles manifest in ways that interfere with *your* performance. When you address the issue (and you will), you easily maintain courteous respect. Having faced your own foibles, you recognize that you and she are, after all, just human beings dealing with some weak links inside.

# A Guiding Framework

"It seems so obvious now when I look at the Chain, but I could never figure out before why I was struggling so much."
—Brandon, technology consultant

The Productivity Chain provides a framework for understanding what makes people productive, and how you can improve your own productivity. This frame gives you a higher perspective, which helps you process new information and, ultimately, spend your self-improvement resources wisely. You can:

Use the Chain to See the Bigger Picture

Any productivity-related factor—from addiction to work ethic—has a place in relation to the Productivity Chain. Most fall within a specific link. A few, such as leadership, are called Link Leapers because they involve the entire Chain. A good leader is personally productive and empowers others to amplify that productivity. Every link in the Chain comes into play when one leads a family, group, or conglomerate.

The image of the Chain on page 45 lists the many productivity terms next to their corresponding links. You can read about many of them in Appendix C: *Productivity-Related Terms* to see how they fit together and into the bigger picture—and what role they may play in your own productivity.

Two factors merit special consideration. The first is mindfulness. Mindfulness positively enhances every link in the Chain (see *Preface* for more details), but, unlike Link Leapers, it is not affected by the links. You might think of it as a Chain booster.

Context, on the other hand, is where the Chain operates. It is the culture (yours and your stakeholders', your organization, country, etc.), the social and political climate, the economic environment, and the ideologies that undergird them all. It is, in other words, the factors around and within you and your Chain. They call can affect your productivity, sometimes in ways beyond your control. You have power only to function as best as possible within the constraints of context.

Use the Chain to Filter Information

Every day brings new ideas, opinions, videos, research, tips, apps, and strategies related to productivity, "organizing," health, communication, and so on—every link in the Chain. You can make sense of it all by filtering it through the Productivity Chain perspective. You might categorize the resources by link or perhaps by using the additional terms listed on page 45. Organizing the data by this framework may help you to decide what to read, believe, and apply.

Use the Chain to Spend Resources Wisely

It makes sense to improve your productivity in the most efficient, effective way. To spend your (or your organization's) money and time wisely, target the resources that will strengthen your weakest links. Your strong links will flourish further when they are no longer hampered by your (formerly) weak ones. (See Appendix D: *Productivity-Related Resources* for suggestions by link.)

7: A GUIDING FRAMEWORK

Mapping Productivity-Related Terms on the Productivity Chain

The Chain below shows productivity-related terms pointing towards their relevant links. There are some factors that involve all the links—these "Link-Leapers" appear at the bottom. The words with asterisks are described in Appendix C: *Productivity-Related Terms*. The rest can be found in the chapter named for their particular link.

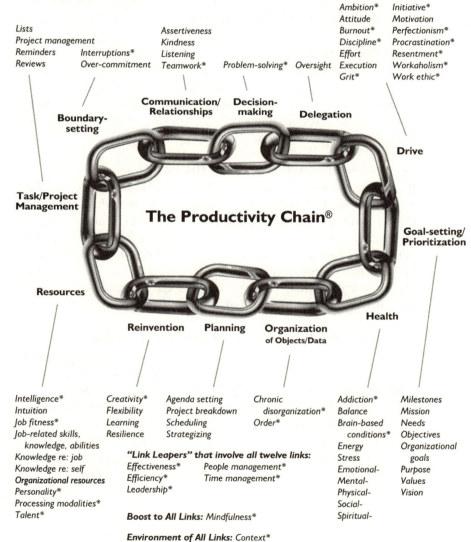

Your Next Step: Depends on You

If you have come this far through the book, you may be at a crossroads. To help you spend your professional development time wisely, here are your options at a glance. See which applies to you and then take action. If you like the stories, don't forget the case study at the end of each section (the first is on the next page).

"I'm ready to go!"

If you want to put down this book and get to work analyzing your Chain, strengthening your weak links, and becoming more productive, have at it! There's no time like the present. I'd love to hear about your journey. You can contact me at *www.CaseyMooreInc.com*.

"I want to learn more about these links."

If you want to learn more, read the next section of this book, *The Twelve Links*. It describes the links in depth, including how each affects your productivity (and other links) and how you can strengthen each. Understanding the links more fully enables you to better assess your own strengths and weaknesses—not just now, but in the future, as your links change. The last section, *Productivity Myths*, offers suggestions and stories about strengthening your links, as well.

"I'm not sure I 'buy' this Productivity Chain."

If you have doubts about the Productivity Chain, that's a fair position. It could be, however, that you have some beliefs about productivity that get in the way of your embracing it. Section III: *Productivity Myths* explores twelve common perspectives that actually inhibit productivity. You might read them to see if any apply to you. And, of course, you don't have to accept or apply the model. I do encourage you to try it out before rejecting it entirely. Your own experience may be the best evidence of its efficacy.

CASE STUDY: DOUGLAS

Douglas' Story

Douglas' Productivity Chain story reveals how the definitions of productivity problems determines their solutions. He thought he needed to get "more organized." He actually needed to address a few productivity factors he had not even considered. When he did, his output increased and his confidence grew.

SUMMARY

The Professional: Douglas is a financial advisor

Strong Links: Boundary-setting, Goal-setting/Prioritization, Health, Task/Project Management

Solutions that Worked—Strengthening the Weak Links:

- Communication/Relationships: Develop assertiveness skills to turn manager and assistant into better supports.
- Planning: Schedule appointments to do time- and focus-intensive activities, such as financial plan analyses.
- Reinvention: Accept and embrace changes in business model.

Douglas, a financial advisor at one of the nation's top banks, had a large and lucrative portfolio. So large, in fact, that it got to be too much. He worked as long and hard as he could, but still could not give his clients the care he once had.

He felt convinced that getting more organized would solve the problem. A thorough assessment, however, revealed that Douglas could locate documents, both digital and paper, in seconds. His systems made sense to himself and to the people who had to access them. Aside from a couple of short, categorized piles on his desk, his office was uncluttered. Organization of Objects/Data was not his problem.

Something was wrong, though, and it turned out to be his Communication/Relationships, Planning, and Reinvention links. When he improved these, his productivity and attitude turned around.

A few changes had sparked his productivity crunch. First, greater success. "I think over the last couple of years I grew too rapidly and I just didn't know how to juggle all the balls,"

THE PRODUCTIVITY CHAIN

he explains. "I felt I couldn't afford to spend any time on certain accounts because there were other, bigger opportunities to work on. So I lost some. I'd think 'I put a lot of energy and effort into getting that account. Why be so dumb to let it go? Fit it into your schedule!'" But he didn't.

In addition, his professional support system lost capacity. His supervisor, the regional manager, retired. He did not like his replacement, a young guy fresh from business school. In addition, his assistant Leticia "had some issues with health and her kid and financial stuff." To escape Leticia's negative attitude, Douglas began doing certain tasks himself, adding to his already-full workload.

Finally, something had to give. "I took a hard look at myself because I knew I was in trouble mentally," Douglas says. "I wasn't happy with anything." That prompted him to get help. "I needed to be honest with myself so I could mentally survive another ten years in this business, and still have a family and still be happy, enjoying all that I have.

"If I had not made any changes, I don't know that I could have lasted. And now I think I could work forever. I'm happy with a lot more things today than I was then," he explains.

The turnaround began with practical new habits. First, he strengthened his Planning link. "I started allocating time for whatever I needed to do, just as I would for a client meeting. I am pretty good about sticking to it."

> *Ultimately, I had to discard a bunch of stuff that was not productive.*
> — Douglas, financial advisor

He gave those task "appointments" his full attention, a practice he continues. "When I'm working on something that has a dedicated time line, I'll minimize the email and it's like, 'All right. This is what I'm working on.' There's nothing else. I'll use the Do Not Disturb button on my phone now. I close my door.

"I never used to do all that. No matter what the interruption was, I always dealt with it immediately. Now I deal with it in an appropriate time, but I focus and I work on whatever needs to be done first." In this way, Douglas' Boundary-setting link cooperated with his Planning link.

CASE STUDY: DOUGLAS

Next, he embraced change—something his weak Reinvention link had caused him to avoid. He adopted a more streamlined business model. "Ultimately, I had to discard a bunch of stuff that was not productive," he admits. That included some clients. "Before, I had more clients and got paid less for each. Now I have fewer and get paid more [for each]. I had three hundred clients and now I'm at forty."

Letting go of his old ways had many rewards. "My annual pay is not quite what it was but it's almost there," he says. The benefits of less stress, fewer to-do's, and the time to serve his clients better more than made up the monetary difference. (Since first edition: He now earns significantly more than ever.)

Finally, Douglas strengthened his Communication/Relationships link by focusing on his own behavior, rather than trying to change his supervisor or assistant. He initiated some frank, direct conversations with his new manager. As a result, "my feelings towards him have dramatically changed for the better," he reports, "And I've seen more respect from him to me." He now views his supervisor as a source of support, not stress, strengthening his Drive link.

> I've instituted more happiness in my life.
> Douglas, financial advisor

He also began taking charge of his communications with Leticia. "'Woe is me' is her attitude," Douglas explains. "I cut that right out of the conversation. I don't want to hear the negativity or the political stuff that goes on at the branch. I don't want that to pollute my mind." Instead of avoiding her, however, Douglas redirects the subject so politely that Leticia has no idea her complaints are being shut down.

The focusing on communication has made Douglas a better listener. "I'm trying to understand people better and play off of them, rather than always trying to make my points," he says.

With the weak links in his Productivity Chain fortified, Douglas' performance at work once again meets his own standards. His perspective on his life has also improved. "I've instituted more happiness in my life," he smiles. "I've also added a grandson. Now I leave work early sometimes so I can see the little fellow. I enjoy that." Improving his weak links improved the social aspect of his Health link, too.

Section II
The Twelve Links

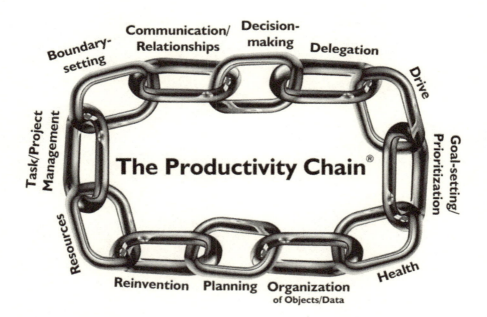

The Twelve Links Introduction

"Knowledge is power."
—Sir Francis Bacon

Each link in the Productivity Chain represents a rich and complex set of knowledge, skills, and abilities. Each contributes to, or detracts from, your overall effectiveness at work—and life. Experts devote entire books, videos, websites, and careers to the topics encompassed in a single link, such as Health, or just one aspect of a link, such as attitude (part of the Drive link).

This section does not attempt to say everything there is to say about each link. That would take volumes. Instead, each chapter that follows:

- describes a given link's important features and effects on productivity;
- tells at least one story of someone improving that link;
- outlines concrete strategies for strengthening that particular link so you can take immediate action, if necessary;
- gives examples of how that link interacts with the other links in the Chain (in a box on the last page of each chapter).

The section concludes with suggested next steps and a case study. It lists the links in alphabetical order for easy reference. No link is more important than another. From your standpoint, though, the most important links are probably those you need to strengthen within yourself.

THE PRODUCTIVITY CHAIN

Apply the Links to Yourself

Learning about the links is not an academic exercise. It helps you recognize your own strengths and weaknesses and therefore better apply the Productivity Chain Analysis described in Chapter 4: *Identify Solutions* to make changes. That is what Butch, the litigation attorney in the case study at the end of this section, did.

As you read, think about your own links, and ask yourself questions such as these:

TAKE ACTION
As you read about the links, assess your own strengths and weaknesses.

- Which of my links are vulnerable or solid?
- How have they changed over time?
- How would strengthening key links help me?

Additional Resources

This book contains resources to deepen your understanding of the twelve links and to help you build relevant skills once you identify your weak areas:

- To assess your links formally, take the Productivity Chain Self-Assessment at *www.CaseyMooreInc.com*. It identifies areas for you to evaluate or explore further.

- To appreciate the mechanism of how your links interact with each other to influence your performance level, see Chapter 2: *How the Productivity Chain Functions*.

- To understand how common productivity-related factors, such as ambition or procrastination, fit into the Productivity Chain model and particular links, see Appendix C: *Productivity-Related Terms*.

- For ideas about the process of strengthening your weak links, see Chapter 5: *Strengthen Your Weak Links*.

- To find other books and resources that explore specific links in depth, see Appendix D: *Productivity-Related Resources*.

Your honest self-reflection, combined with your greater knowledge of the links and how to strengthen them, will give you a blueprint for increasing your productivity—one link at a time.

Link 8

Boundary-setting

"The most useful thing I gained was the realization that it was okay to shut my door, and it was okay to turn my phone off, and it was okay to do what I needed to do rather than what everybody else needed."
 —Anne, executive vice president, telecom company

Boundaries are the limits you set with yourself and others—the mental lines in the sand you draw. In fact, the phrase "crossing the line" refers to unacceptable boundary violations, such as cheating or calling names.

Your boundaries reflect your values, needs, life experiences, and culture. They guide your behavior in ways both mundane ("I do not answer phone calls while meeting with others") and profound ("I will never kill anyone").

Your boundaries may change over time and circumstances. They may be relatively easy for you to maintain at work, but not at home—or vice versa. They might be robust in some respects and barely existent in others; flexible and evolving, or rigid and set. They may be so permeable that you intrude past other people's boundaries without realizing it, or so firm they seem like walls.

This Link Protects You

Your Boundary-setting link protects you and your time, effort, and energy—helping you bypass the distractions that would otherwise delay or prevent you from achieving your goals. The Boundary-setting link includes boundary-maintenance, too.

Ultimately, Boundary-setting consolidates your personal power. It lets you define for yourself what matters to you, what treatment you expect and accept, and how you will spend your time.

Effects of Boundary-setting on Productivity

The importance of effective boundaries to your productivity cannot be overestimated. When your Boundary-setting link is strong enough, it enables you to:

- **Keep commitments manageable.** Boundaries help you determine which commitments to accept. When over-extended, your production may be high but it is unsustainable. You get stretched thin, as Crystal, a solo entrepreneur, discovered. That's why she began setting more robust boundaries.

    "I get so many invitations—'come do this,' 'come do that,'" she explains. "But I am getting better at saying 'no.' My fear is becoming that person who doesn't do anything. But I've got to look at it in terms of blocks of time or phases of life. I'm really clear on what I want to accomplish with my new business, so I have to focus on that."

- **Manage interruptions.** Firm but flexible boundaries help you prevent, minimize, and effectively handle unnecessary interruptions (including self-interruptions). They help you work efficiently.

    Tom, a healthcare executive, limits phone calls so he can focus on the task at hand. "I've turned off all alerts, but I have it on vibrate when it rings," he says. Caller ID lets him selectively control who can access him and he returns other calls later.

    Teri, who runs a recruiting service, trained her staff to stop interrupting her. "Now they don't attack me as I'm walking in the door," she reports. "They know I put down boundaries on what time I have available for them, but I'm very receptive during that time. We get along better now."

    She experienced the paradox of boundary-setting: When you set reasonable limits to protect your time, others respect them and often find you more approachable. You can be more receptive because you feel more in control. Clear, healthy limits improve relationships.

- **Clarify roles and responsibilities.** Roles and responsibilities are, essentially, boundaries. Healthy boundaries empower you to fulfill your own duties. You may help coworkers, direct-reports, supervisors, even your children, with their work at

8: BOUNDARY-SETTING LINK

times, but you do not take on their responsibilities as your own. Instead, you respect their right to learn and grow, achieve and fail, and experience consequences of their actions or inaction—just as you do yourself.

- **Preserve emotional calm and protect other links.** Boundary-setting keeps you from being taken advantage of by others. No one can "use you" without your permission, of course, but if your Boundary-setting link is weak, you may feel you cannot say "no." You lack power.

When in that position, you may be annoyed at the person in question, affecting your Communication/Relationships link. Over time, that irritation can harden into resentment, impairing your energy and motivation (your Drive link). A strong enough Boundary-setting link avoids all that, preserving your integrity and peace of mind.

> Love your neighbor, yet pull not down your hedge.
> *George Herbert*

Irene's Boundary-setting Story

Irene, a director of quality assurance, began minding other people's business—a boundary-busting habit. She contacted me because, while she achieved most of her goals, she had to work long hours and many weekends to do it. When we discussed her many responsibilities, it became clear that several actually belonged to Magda, another director.

Irene had assumed these duties over time. Magda "couldn't handle" this one, so Irene took it on. When Magda got sick and missed work, as she often did, Irene stepped in. Employees found Magda difficult and unhelpful, so they called Irene instead.

The few times Irene asked Magda to do more, Magda cried and carried on. Eventually, Irene gave up. She also kept the problem to herself, not wanting to get Magda "in trouble" with her boss.

Irene had the best of intentions. She wanted to pitch in and do what was needed for the good of the company. But as her own responsibilities increased, she had to stop "helping."

She realized that covering for Magda hurt the organization. Irene met her goals—barely—but had no time to exceed them. She risked becoming burned out and quitting. Losing her would damage the business much more than losing Magda.

After realizing that her weak Boundary-setting link was the reason for her predicament, Irene took action. She started minding her own business and letting Magda mind hers. When Magda missed work, for example, Irene let Magda's boss figure out how to take up the slack. When employees called her with a Magda matter, she gently referred them to Magda herself.

Once they began to get complaints about Magda, senior executives realized the problem. They didn't fire her, but they did hire someone to help both Magda and Irene. Irene's job became manageable once again.

How to Strengthen Your Boundary-setting Link

If your Productivity Chain Analysis indicates you need to strengthen your Boundary-setting link, you might begin with these suggestions:

Make an internal commitment.

The most important boundary-setting occurs within yourself. ***You*** determine what you find acceptable (or not) and commit to that limit. "I won't go back to putting orders in," states Alan, a sales consultant. "I won't go back to staying late anymore. I won't go back to working on the weekends. I started putting in these little thresholds that I won't pass. I made a commitment."

What is most important about these commitments is that Alan made them to ***himself***. They enable him to make his external actions reflect his internal boundaries.

Remember: When you say "yes" to one thing, you say "no" to something else.

You can't be in two places at one time. If you work late to please a client, you can't have dinner with the family. If you join that softball team, you have to leave work early on Thursdays.

Whatever you decide, be conscious of the trade-off you are making. The trade-off may involve people, not just activities or projects. If you say "yes" to please a colleague, for instance, you

8: BOUNDARY-SETTING LINK

may end up displeasing your spouse, your child, your boss—or yourself.

Carleen, a graphic designer, found that saying "no" or "not this time" to some people freed her to focus her time more productively and enjoyably. "Certain clients have drained me of time, energy, and resources and I'm not letting them do it anymore," she says. "It's about quality, not quantity."

> A "no" uttered from the deepest conviction is better than a "yes" merely uttered to please or, what is worse, to avoid trouble.
> — Mahatma Gandhi

She let go of some difficult clients and quickly found more agreeable replacements. She also found that raising her rates—another boundary—eliminated tiny jobs that demanded more time than they were worth.

Mind your own business.

Minding your own business means letting other people solve their own problems. Of course, helping others during particularly difficult times is a kindness, especially if they ask for assistance. Assuming their responsibilities on a regular basis, however, is not—as Irene discovered.

Consistently doing for others what they could (or should) do for themselves decreases **your** productivity and crosses boundaries. It may seem "nice," but it actually sends the message that those you "help" are inadequate or incompetent. In the end, it hurts you, the other person, and the entire organization.

Close the door sometimes.

An open-door policy is a philosophy—a statement of open-mindedness and willingness to listen and help. It is not a promise of unlimited and immediate access.

If you need to work on something that requires concentration, close your office door or go work in the conference room. Go off-site if necessary. Tell your colleagues you need an hour without disturbance unless the building is on fire. Then turn off the phone and email. You'll be amazed at what you accomplish. Then you can return to being available with peace of mind.

If you workplace offers no refuge, consider changing your hours to work an hour before everyone else arrives or after they go home.

THE PRODUCTIVITY CHAIN

How Your Boundary-setting Link Interacts with Other Links

Here are examples of how this link interacts with the other eleven:

Communication/Relationships: Defending boundaries requires speaking up when lines are crossed. Clear, consistent, and appropriate boundaries form the sound container for healthy relationships.

Decision-making: Boundary-setting and -maintenance begins with a decision to set or defend.

Delegation: Holding staff accountable for their performance requires drawing a line between supervisor and direct-report.

Drive: Shutting down an inner perfectionist or procrastinator requires firm mental boundaries.

Goal-setting/Prioritization: Knowing your goals, values, and priorities helps you say "no" or "not now" to the people, interruptions, opportunities, and distractions that might interfere with achieving those goals.

Health: Setting limits with yourself (to take a break or leave work, for instance) enables you to manage your energy and maintain your health.

Organization of Objects/Data: Discarding an object, paper, or email means saying "no" and committing to that limit.

Planning: Scheduling appointments or milestones creates boundary lines on your calendar. Boundary-setting enables you to enforce those plans by not letting other activities trespass onto them unless you consciously decide it's warranted.

Reinvention: Modifying your boundaries to fit the people, your relationship with them, and the circumstances is important. It reflects an ability to adapt flexibly to change.

Resources: Setting boundaries enables you to protect your area's critical tools, equipment, personnel, and so on, when competition for organizational resources exists.

Task/Project Management: Distinguishing between tasks and projects draws a boundary line between the two. That clarity ensures that your projects move forward one action at a time.

Link 9

Communication/ Relationships

"I would fight for things for selfish reasons. When I stopped that, the way people treated me changed in a huge way. They saw I was looking out for the company—not making them work extra hard just for me. So they were inclined to do a lot more for me."
—Alan, sales consultant

The glue binding your relationships with others is communication. It sets—and reflects—the tone and depth of your relationships. Communication and relationships are distinct concepts, yet they are so entwined they form one link in the Productivity Chain.

Clear communication ensures that the right work gets performed the right way. In the context of the Productivity Chain, "communication" refers to exchanging meaning through listening, speaking, reading, writing, actions, and demeanor.

"Relationships" include your connections with coworkers of all levels, clients, prospects, colleagues, vendors, friends, and family. All these people can support or inhibit your productivity, depending on your relationship with them.

This Link Connects You

Your Communication/Relationships link connects you with other people. Building positive, functional connections with others enables you to accomplish much more than you could alone.

Your productivity depends on your ability to enlist others to help you achieve your goals, if only by providing access or information. This influence is an important part of your personal power. When you inspire people and win their trust, your productivity swells from the combined output of those around you.

Components of Communication that Affect Productivity

Communication involves more than speaking and listening. Our very presence and way of being conveys a lot. The following aspects of communication that affect relationships and productivity.

- **Listening:** Communication only occurs when a message is received and understood. Good listening makes it possible.

- **Message:** Your message includes the *explicit* content you want to convey, as well as the *implicit* messages you send (either deliberately or inadvertently). You may not realize you send implicit messages, but everyone does.

- **Mode:** You probably convey your overt messages in two common modes—orally (e.g., face-to-face, by phone, through video) or in writing (e.g., email, texts, letters, reports, slideshows, and other documents). The mode matters. Firing an employee by email or text, for example, conveys disrespect far more than many words spoken face-to-face would.

- **Delivery:** The delivery includes your word choice, tone, facial expression, emotional intensity, appearance, dress, body language, and so on. Your demeanor sends signals.

- **Timing:** *When* you deliver a message has meaning. Responding to a client within the hour says one thing; responding two days later says another. Providing relevant data in a timely manner promotes productivity; waiting until it's too late does not.

- **Recipient(s):** *Who* gets included in a communication exchange is significant. You may address a person's supervisor, rather than the individual himself, for example. You may invite someone to a meeting—or not. Witnesses matter, too. Speaking to someone with others present or copying (even blind-copying) others on an email alters the message's implicit meaning.

- **Context:** Every communication occurs within larger contexts. These include the situation the message addresses; the culture and current climate—perhaps influenced by recent events—of your organization, profession, city, state, country; and the background and personality of the other person(s) involved.

9: COMMUNICATION/RELATIONSHIPS LINK

- **Behavior:** Actions speak more loudly than words. You can **say** that you want to hear your executive team's ideas, for example, but if you "listen" to your COO while texting a friend, you tell your COO that he is not important or that you cannot control your own impulses.

> *What you do speaks so loudly that I cannot hear what you say.*
> Ralph Waldo Emerson

You earn credibility and respect from others when your listen actively and your mode, delivery, timing, recipients, context, and behavior are all consistent with your explicit message.

Components of Relationships that Affect Productivity

Productive professional relationships involve respect, reciprocity, and team-orientation. Liking everyone is not required; treating everyone respectfully is. Aspects of relationships that affect communication and productivity include:

- **Your value:** How people relate to you depends in part on your value to them, which, in turn, depends on how you treat them and on how well you perform for them. A kind, winning personality is not enough; you must be competent and trustworthy to gain loyal allies.

- **Your friendships:** Friendships with coworkers may help your productivity—when, for example, they go the extra mile for you. Friendships can also hinder your effectiveness—when, for instance, you find it difficult to hold a coworker friend accountable for fear of damaging your personal relationship with him.

- **Others' relationships:** Others' relationships (including friendships, romantic involvements, and family relations) may affect how you interact with them. You may be reluctant to set tough boundaries with someone who goes fishing with the CEO, for instance.

- **Avoidance:** You may go to elaborate lengths to avoid dealing with a toxic, incompetent, or otherwise difficult person. This damaged relationship can affect an entire organization's performance, especially if you put others in the middle.

Navigating professional and personal relationships successfully requires awareness and openness. Direct communication helps. Instead of making assumptions or trying to figure out how to "handle" someone, for instance, ask that person what *she* prefers. Relationships have two sides, after all.

Effects of Communication/Relationships on Productivity

When you use clear, direct communication and cultivate healthy, positive relationships, your Communication/Relationships link is strong enough and you can:

- **Achieve greater accuracy.** Clear and direct communication ensures the right people do the right work the right way at the right time. "Clear" and "direct" are the key words here. People may understand what you *say*, but what you *mean* may be open for interpretation. Effective communication occurs when all parties agree on meaning. It increases accuracy, prevents wasted time, and usually improves relationships.

- **Attract better ideas and information.** Clear and direct communication makes other people feel emotionally safe and professionally valued—encouraging them to share their best ideas about improving operations, service, products, and so on.

    In addition, people usually like and respect those who treat them with respect and appreciation. They share with them valuable information, including warnings of potential problems. The ideas and information that flow to you when you communicate well increase your overall productivity.

- **Obtain more resources.** When you foster healthy relationships, you gain access to resources that are not available to people with weaker interpersonal skills, as Jaiden found.

Jaiden's Story

Jaiden headed purchasing for a manufacturing company. Over the years, he built positive associations with vendors across the country. When he needed a rush order, his suppliers were happy to help. Recently, a run on a specific material created scarcity nationwide. Jaiden's factory never experienced a hiccup

9: COMMUNICATION/RELATIONSHIPS LINK

in production because his allies put him at the top of their distribution lists. His genuine interest in them paid dividends.

- **Improve others' performance.** When you communicate your high expectations to others, they often rise to meet them.

Sheila's Story

Sheila, a public relations director, liked Tim, one of her PR reps, but doubted his capacity to really succeed. Tim often said his workload was too much and Sheila spent lots of time and energy trying to help him cope.

As a result of our coaching, Sheila agreed to treat Tim as if he *were* fully competent. Over the next few weeks, when Tim complained, she would calmly reply, "I know you're up to the challenge," or something similar.

In time, Tim *did* start meeting the challenge. "We just went through one of the busiest seasons we've had so far," Sheila reports. "Tim stayed on top of everything. The old Tim would have crumbled." Sheila communicated her confidence in Tim and he performed accordingly. Their relationship, and their joint productivity, improved dramatically as a result.

Darryl's Communication/Relationships Story

Darryl was the new CEO of a company whose board wielded considerable power. To forge a positive working relationship, Darryl went out of his way to meet the sometimes unreasonable demands of the board's Chairperson, even setting aside more important activities to do so.

He also worked long hours. He wanted to communicate that he was as committed to the business as the Chair, a workaholic with a seventy-hours-a-week habit. As a result, Darryl, an avid cyclist, had not ridden his bike in months.

His sense of integrity felt shaken because, while he valued and believed in work-life integration, he no longer practiced it. He asked me to coach him, recognizing he had a deeper problem than lack of exercise. After realizing his weak links were Health, Boundary-setting, and Communication/Relationships, Darryl decided to take action. First, he began cycling again. Soon after, he felt empowered to change his relationship with the Chair, as well.

A small incident marked a turning point. The Chair had scheduled a meeting for a time when Darryl's shared calendar indicated he was not available. In the past, Darryl would have cancelled his other appointment. Not this time. He communicated directly and clearly—explaining the situation, expressing his regrets, and offering to meet later to discuss what he had missed.

He smiled as he relayed the story of asserting himself this way. Months ago, he had handed his personal power to the Chair. This time, with a polite "no," Darryl reclaimed that power for himself. He communicated that he had his own priorities and was an equal partner in their relationship.

> With a polite "no," Darryl communicated that he had his own priorities and was an equal partner in their relationship.

At the time, the Chair directed his annoyance at his assistant, who had made the scheduling error. He seemed to respect Darryl more, however, and that respect grew as Darryl began standing up more often for what he believed. Darryl's self-respect grew, too.

He began communicating a new message to his direct-reports, one that paved a way for "a healthier organization" in more ways than one. He modeled self-care by taking time to exercise and encouraged others to do the same. He also rewarded authenticity, inviting employees to share ideas and ask for what they needed.

Changing an organization's culture is difficult, but Darryl believes he is on the right path. "Productivity and creativity thrive when people feel confident, rather than cowed," he says.

How to Strengthen Your Communication/Relationships Link

Improving your communication can strengthen your relationships. Stronger relationships can ease communication. Both influence your overall productivity directly and through their effect on other links. If your Productivity Chain Analysis indicates you need to strengthen your Communication/Relationships link, you might begin with these suggestions:

Speak and write assertively.

Assertive communication is the most effective way to convey your ideas and get the results you seek. It is direct, open, and clear—

9: COMMUNICATION/RELATIONSHIPS LINK

based on the premise that everyone deserves respect. By definition, it is never aggressive, abusive, passive, manipulative, or underhanded. It is impersonal, open, and nonviolent.

If you do not communicate assertively most of the time, find a book, class, or expert to help you learn how. (For suggestions, see Chapter 5: *Strengthen Your Weak Links* and Appendix D: *Productivity-Related Resources*.)

Listen well.

Listening attentively and respectfully builds relationships and trust. The quality of your listening determines what you perceive, receive, and understand. It helps you avoid problems and learn about opportunities.

> *The single biggest problem in communication is the illusion that it has taken place.*
> — George Bernard Shaw

So put down the phone or your pen, dim your computer screen, and give the person before you (or on the phone) your full attention.

Communicate often.

In this world of overload, your clients and coworkers want to know their email, voicemail, or text has not been lost in your shuffle. Fortunately, you do not have to fully respond to every communication instantly to reassure them.

You can minimize their "just checking" messages by acknowledging requests within a timeframe you decide. A quick email saying simply, "I got your message; will answer by Friday." reassures the other person that you are aware and they matter. It also helps you prioritize and plan, taking the perceived urgency level down a notch.

Be kind.

You have probably been told since childhood to be "nice." As you know, niceness is pretty superficial. For many people, it means "don't make waves" or "be pleasant to get what you want." Kindness, however, comes from within. It is an expression of respect and caring for our shared humanity.

Being kind doesn't mean being a pushover. Kindness actually allows you to hold people accountable—which some think isn't "nice"—while maintaining positive relationships with them. Speaking up when a colleague fails to meet commitments shows that you respect the person and that her work matters.

Kindness can be difficult to muster in trying circumstances. It helps to remember that it is a learned behavior, not an emotion. Here are two suggestions to make it a habit:

- **Practice kindness with everyone.** Say "hello" to the receptionist. Remember your coworker's birthday. Scott, a commercial real estate agent, built a positive connection with the department's administrative assistant and reaped the rewards of making genuinely kind requests.

  "The other people ***demand*** things of her, and I ***ask*** things of her," he says. "I approach her in a courteous way, and she'd do anything for me. She puts my work first because I treat her well." He treats her well out of authentic respect, not as a means of manipulation. Treating others kindly makes him feel good.

- **Assume goodwill in others.** When someone does something that seems silly, irresponsible, or "wrong," pause. You can access your kindness—and avoid a rush to judgment—by considering alternative interpretations with this exercise.

Exercise: Three Good Reasons

Think of three reasons an intelligent, well-intentioned person might have done such a thing. Maybe a loved one died and his brain is fogged with grief, for example. Maybe he had a brain tumor that impaired his judgment. Maybe he was given bad information.

> **TAKE ACTION**
> Do the "Three Good Reasons" exercise to stay kind even when it's difficult.

Then take a deep breath. Whatever the real story, you can now address the person with kind respect because you've changed your own perspective—or at least reminded yourself that your initial viewpoint isn't the only one. This exercise makes you more receptive to hearing other people's side of the story—an opening for real communication.

Practiced consistently, kindness enables you to build functional relationships that support and enhance your productivity.

9: COMMUNICATION/RELATIONSHIPS LINK

How Your Communication/Relationships Link Interacts with Other Links

Here are examples of how this link interacts with the other eleven:

Boundary-setting: Defending boundaries requires speaking up when lines are crossed. Clear, consistent, and appropriate boundaries form the sound container for healthy relationships.

Decision-making: Communicating effectively and building cooperative relationships both begin with decisions regarding what to say, how to say it, to whom, when, and so on.

Delegation: Leading and managing teams depends greatly on building positive relationships and communicating effectively.

Drive: Communicating your attitude to others is inevitable. Positive or negative, your attitude affects how people relate to you. Their recurring attitudes influence your outlook and relationships with them, as well.

Goal-setting/Prioritization: Inspiring others to help you achieve your (and your organization's) goals requires persuasive communication and influence in the relationships.

Health: Developing a network of family, friends, and/or compatible people increases your social health, which may translate into better mental and physical health. Communicating clearly with medical professionals can benefit your health, as well.

Organization of Objects/Data: Organizing your work area makes you feel more comfortable with inviting others in. It makes others confident that they can leave notes or send messages without fear they will be lost.

Planning: Planning often involves other people, requiring clear communication and cooperative relationships.

Reinvention: Embracing or resisting change may alter your relationships with others, depending on their approaches to the situation.

Resources: Communicating assertively enables you to request and obtain necessary training and resources. Leveraging relationships may be a resource, as well.

Task/Project Management: Many projects involve other people and success depends upon clear communication and positive relationships, just so they'll share information if nothing else.

Link

 **Decision-making**

"I say, 'If you've got to know the answer right now, the answer is no. Let me think about it and get back with you.' That gives me space to make a non-emotional decision."
—Butch, litigation attorney

Deciding what to do, when to do it, and how best to do it is the foundation of productivity. It affects many links in the Productivity Chain directly, and is a skill set in its own right.

Some decisions have little consequence; others change your life or seal your company's fate. Most fall somewhere in between. To be effective, decision-making on any level must be appropriately thoughtful and timely. Poor, rash, or unnecessarily delayed decision-making creates bottlenecks and disorder.

This Link Activates Your Work

Your Decision-making link activates your work by triggering your other links. Deciding what matters most enables you to set goals and prioritize (Goal-setting/Prioritization link). Deciding what to keep and where to keep it paves the way for a stronger Organization of Objects/Data link. Deciding how to respond is the "prep work" for handling an email (Task/Project Management link). And so on.

Decision-making falls completely within your control and determines your behavior and perspective. It therefore unleashes or inhibits your personal power.

Decision-making Solves Problems

Management authority Peter Drucker classified decision-making as

10: DECISION-MAKING LINK

a form of problem-solving.¹ The problem might be "how can we keep the company growing in an increasingly fragmented market?" or it might be "what is the highest and best use of my time for the next ten minutes?"

Many factors affect decision-making, including how you define your problem (see Chapter 3: *A Powerful Perspective*), the quality and availability of information at your disposal, your decision-making process itself, the players involved in that particular decision, and your personal style.

> *A life spent in making mistakes is not only more honorable but more useful than a life spent doing nothing.*
> George Bernard Shaw

Some people make decisions too quickly, and their impulsive choices lead to unwelcome results. Others decide much more slowly, researching their options to the point of "analysis paralysis." Both extremes cause difficulties. Successful decision-making requires giving a matter the amount of consideration its importance merits.

Effects of Decision-making on Productivity

As the box on link interactions at the end of this chapter reveals, action in every area of the Chain begins with a decision. When your Decision-making link is strong enough, you:

- **Guide your business profitably.** Your business decisions determine your organization's success. Deciding to pursue this customer, use that vendor, purchase this equipment, expand that line, or hire this person could take your profits from $20,000 to $20 million—productivity increases. On the other hand, poor decisions could land your organization in bankruptcy—productivity ceases.

    Sound decision-making requires information and expertise you either possess or need to acquire (through your Resources link). Whatever your position in your organization, your value to it comes at least in part from your ability to make such decisions successfully.

- **Use your time profitably.** As productivity expert Brian Tracy writes, "Time management is control over what you do next."² It is, in other words, a decision you make each moment. Wise decisions help you use your time profitably. Unwise decisions make your time unproductive or even counterproductive. In that case, fortunately, you can make a different choice the next moment.

You decision-making affects many links directly; that's why it is key to your performance. Each day, you decide what to do, how to do it, who should do it, when to do it, and what to do with it until then or after that. In order, those decisions relate to your Goal-setting/Prioritization, Task/Project Management, Delegation, Planning, and Organization of Objects/Data links.

- **Use others' time profitably.** Whether you are a CEO, assistant, or spouse, your decision-making affects those around you. You can improve their productivity by making decisions in a timely way so they don't have to wait for you. Delaying a decision becomes a *de facto* decision, albeit a passive one. Opportunities pass and options close as time passes.

  Avoiding a decision is very different from deliberately deciding to take no action at present. Some situations do resolve themselves and deliberate delay can be wise, as diplomats and negotiators know.

Ashley's Decision-making Story

A productivity truism states that every pile of clutter represents decisions to be made.[3] Ashley, a chief operations officer, had many such piles. Her Organization of Objects/Data link was weak, but her Decision-making link was even weaker—hence the clutter.

Her email in-box contained 5,000 unfiled emails, many of them marked unread. Carefully-separated mounds of files and loose papers lined her desk, the floor behind it, and her bookshelves. She had many decisions to make.

The sheer weight of all those unresolved matters paralyzed her, so she called me for help. In two intense days, Ashley made hundreds of decisions. She found it exhilarating and exhausting. Her goal: clear the decks so she could focus on her most important work.

First, she made the difficult but liberating decision to review only the relatively current items. She tossed many old papers wholesale, knowing she hadn't touched them in years. Most were

10: DECISION-MAKING LINK

Exercise: Play the "A" Game

To make decisions about the objects and information in your world, it helps to keep it simple and limit your action choices.

1. **Assess:** Determine what you've got in hand or on screen. Is it work or personal? What objective does it serve?
2. **Act:** Pick the course of action from these options:

   Accomplish: Do it now or later, depending on its priority.
   Assign: Delegate it to someone else.
   Abandon: Toss or delete it.
   Archive: File it for future reference.

---

obsolete or available digitally, anyway.

She also moved the majority of her emails (60 days or older) into a folder called "Old Emails." She kept them because some certainly should be kept. Reviewing each one again to find the few she needed would waste time, however.

Over the course of those two days, Ashley decided how to handle her remaining papers and emails using the "'A' Game" exercise (see box above). She would use the same method to process her work going forward. When she couldn't decide something immediately, she added it to her task list so she wouldn't forget to make a final decision.

> Ashley made the difficult but liberating decision to review only the relatively current items.

Once time had passed, Ashley could more clearly see how her indecision had affected her and others. "Before, I was definitely less productive," she admits. "It spilled onto my coworkers. They couldn't get their jobs accomplished because they were waiting for something from me. I was holding up multiple people—but not anymore." These days, she makes decisions about each piece of paper and email soon after it arrives.

How to Strengthen Your Decision-making Link

Decision-making has a profound impact on your productivity, but people often take it for granted. If your Productivity Chain Analysis indicates you need to strengthen your Decision-making link, you might begin with these suggestions:

Limit your options.

Limiting your options can ease decision-making, especially when the decision's consequences are not life and death. Researchers witnessed this effect in a jam-selling experiment.

Customers were more likely to ***visit*** a table with twenty-four types of jams on it, but ten times more likely to ***buy*** when only six flavors were displayed. The researchers concluded that too many options immobilizes decision-making.[4] Get your Boundary-setting link involved and limit yourself to three to five options and then choose one.

Limit your time.

Some decisions have serious consequences and merit deep consideration. Others do not. You can take control of your decision-making by clarifying the importance of the decision you need to make. If it is high, setting (and sharing) a realistic deadline to make your choice can help you avoid analysis paralysis.

When it comes to relatively inconsequential decisions, such as where to store a document in your office, force yourself to decide quickly. The sooner you decide, the sooner you realize the effects of your decision, and the sooner you can course-correct if need be.

Talk or write about it.

It may help to discuss the situation with a trusted colleague—not so much to get their advice, as to help you sort out your own thoughts. Putting your ideas onto paper helps in a similar way—it stops the mental running in circles. Set aside what you have written and read it later. The time away creates enough distance to increase your objectivity when you read what you wrote.

Trust your intuition.

Tapping into your intuition can aid decision-making at times. As security expert Gavin deBecker points out in his book, *The Gift of Fear*, however, deciphering your intuition's message is a learned skill.[5]

10: DECISION-MAKING LINK

Rather than trust your "gut feeling" blindly, use your logical brain to figure out why you have "a bad feeling" about an opportunity or an "instinctive" distrust of someone. Your intuition may have caught legitimate cues and signals that will affect your decision. Your intuition can be a powerful resource when you refine your ability to interpret it.

How Your Decision-making Link Interacts with Other Links

Here are examples of how this link interacts with the other eleven:

Boundary-setting: Boundary-setting and -maintenance begins with a decision to set or defend.

Communication/Relationships: Communicating effectively and building cooperative relationships both begin with decisions regarding what to say, how to say it, to whom, when, and so on.

Delegation: Delegating begins with decisions: what to delegate, to whom, and so on.

Drive: Changing your attitude or level of urgency towards a task requires a decision.

Goal-setting/Prioritization: Goal-setting requires deciding what is important and when. Prioritization is a specific kind of decision-making.

Health: Taking care of your health and balancing your activities requires making decisions every day, many times a day.

Organization of Objects/Data: Organizing requires you to decide what to keep, what to toss, where to keep your objects and data, and for how long.

Planning: Planning begins with decisions: when to schedule what and for how long, what to include in a project plan, and so on.

Reinvention: Reinventing yourself successfully begins with a decision to adapt to new conditions, whether they originate inside you or come from your environment.

Resources: Obtaining additional knowledge, skills, and other resources requires a decision to act.

Task/Project Management: Managing tasks and projects effectively requires constant decisions about what action to take with each document, email, and so on.

Link 11 Delegation

"The delegating was the big thing. I used to do stuff regardless of whether it was my job or not. Now I assign somebody to do it, and then make sure they actually do it, rather than just taking the "easy way" and doing it myself. It made me start using people for what they were paid to do."
—Jessica, small business owner

In the strictest sense, to delegate means to give power or authority to someone to act on your behalf. In the workplace, it refers to assigning tasks to direct-reports and others. When it comes to the Productivity Chain, however, delegation has a broader meaning. Enlisting anyone to help you manage your responsibilities, both personal and professional, can be considered delegating.

This Link Values You

Your Delegation link values you and your time. It frees you to focus on your high-worth activities—decisions and duties only you can handle.

When you focus on high-value activities, your organization gets the best return on its investment in you. It doesn't make fiscal sense for you to do tasks that someone paid a tenth of your wages could do, while work that requires your expertise waits, undone.

> When you focus on high-value activities, your organization gets the best return on its investment in you.

Allowing others to help you enhances your personal power because you can then apply it where it has the most influence—on your efforts to achieve your goals and contribute your gifts most fully. Doing less impactful tasks can, at times, divert or stifle your productivity power.

11: DELEGATION LINK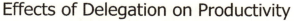

Effects of Delegation on Productivity

Delegation multiplies your productivity—the more people to help, the more results produced. When your Delegation link is strong enough, you can:

- **Do high-yield activities.** By spending more time on matters that demand your level of expertise and experience, you can generate more income or results for the organization. Brandon, a technology consultant, hired an assistant and his productivity increased significantly once the initial adjustment period ended. He spent more time on his clients and his business development efforts while his assistant handled administrative matters.

- **Access more resources and build greater capacity.** Your employees may have stronger skills in some areas, know better ways to do things, and have more time to do them than you. Delegation allows you to access those valuable resources.

  Yes, they will make mistakes. You do, too. With the proper training and oversight, however, their errors will likely not be catastrophic. And the benefits of delegation far exceed the risks of trying to do it all yourself.

  When you see your work with others as an opportunity to mentor and develop them, you take delegation to a new level. You create greater capacity in them—knowledge, skills, and experience that you, and they, can tap later on.

- **Enjoy your work more.** When you let go of non-core responsibilities, you personally benefit. Your own work becomes more appealing because you do more of what interests and challenges you. Building trust and inspiring loyalty in those who report to you is gratifying, too. When you enjoy your work more, your energy level rises along with your sense of purpose, buoying your productivity.

Tony's Delegation Story

Tony, who managed a department of budget analysts, couldn't understand why his staff didn't do what they were told. When the CEO assigned *him* a responsibility, he did it immediately and did it well. He expected the same from his analysts. As good as his people were, however, they were only human and burdened by heavy workloads. They made mistakes occasionally. By the time Tony discovered them, they required a great deal of effort to fix. That's why he called me.

It took a while (and a little convincing) for Tony to let go of the myth that "other people are the problem" (see Chapter 30) and to accept that he played a role in the situation. Finally, he realized that if **he** didn't change, nothing else would. He needed some way to track the work he assigned—to tighten oversight. After some trial and error, he settled on a strategy that fit him and his team.

> Delegate, but participate.

"I make delegation work," he explains, "one, by being clear; two, by having a record of what I assigned; three, by establishing how progress is reported; and four, ensuring compliance. You can't just assume it. That's what I did and it didn't work. I have established protocols where there are successive deadlines to meet. That way, we don't miss or get caught at the last minute."

Tony knew his system worked because fewer errors occurred and he spent less time cleaning up messes. To his surprise, his team actually welcomed his greater oversight. "In a way, they like that I'm looking," he says. "They know I've got the expectation and that I'm backing it up."

He spends more time with them these days, and they now feel safe enough to share—rather than hide—their mistakes. An improved Delegation link strengthened his Communication/Relationships link, as well.

Within a few months, Tony's perspective on delegation had turned 180 degrees from where it began. "I can't just say 'Do it' and expect it to be done every time," he emphasizes today. "Delegation doesn't absolve you of responsibility."

How to Strengthen Your Delegation Link

Improving your Delegation link often involves your Communication/Relationships and Boundary-setting links, as well. If your Productivity Chain Analysis indicates you need to strengthen your Delegation link, you might begin with these suggestions:

11: DELEGATION LINK

Make your expectations clear.

It's all too easy to think that you're on the same page with others, especially if you have worked with them a long time. You expect people to read your mind or have the same standards as you. To exit this road to disappointment, make your expectations clear and explicit.

Describe exactly how you want the finished product to look and when you want it completed. Setting deadlines helps people prioritize. If it makes you uncomfortable, ask the other person to assign *herself* a completion date. You get the deadline you need and she becomes more invested in the project, having taken some ownership of it already. Increase her investment and autonomy by giving her some freedom in **how** she reaches the goal you set.

Build in oversight.

Don't assume, as Tony once did, that if you assign something, it will get done—especially when dealing with unusual tasks or a new person. Delegate, but participate.

Don't participate **too** much, though. Micromanaging—getting over-involved in the details—demoralizes others and wastes your time, so keep your oversight simple. When you assign the task, schedule an appointment to check on its status or set reminders so that you can check in well before the deadline. Keep a "delegated projects" list or flag emailed assignments, so you can track completion.

Cultivate your people.

Yes, you're busy. Still, the more you train those who help you, the more they can take on the tasks that keep you so busy now. Ensure they have the knowledge and resources they need to do their jobs. Share your preferences so they can help you better. Finally, give them opportunities to grow and stretch. People appreciate being challenged. It makes their work more interesting and reflects your confidence in them.

Helping them grow helps you, too. "When I told my assistant to do something the other day, she told me, 'I already started that. I knew that's what you were going to say,'" says Sheila, a director of public relations. "It's amazing how, when you start empowering

THE PRODUCTIVITY CHAIN

people, they do the work without being told." Encouraging your people to stretch their skills and take the initiative keeps them engaged and loyal. And it means less work for you.

Get creative about your delegation options.

Your work situation may not fit the traditional assistant/staff/team model. You may even be the only person in your company right now. Assistant or no assistant, you can still delegate.

Be creative. You can outsource to accountants, bookkeepers, webmasters, tech support, virtual assistants, event organizers, interns, caterers, transcriptionists, concierge services, and so on. Hiring someone to clean your house once a week also counts as delegation—it's anything that frees you to work on your top priorities.

Miguel's Story

Miguel, an office supplies account representative, even delegated the data entry of his customers' sales orders—first to an assistant and then to the customers themselves. "I hired someone to put orders in so I could spend more time with my family," he says. "Now I use her for other things, too: back orders, calling people back, calling people up."

"Before, probably 35 percent of customers ordered online. Now it's close to 80. I encourage them to do it. It makes their lives easier." The result: his assistant could handle more complex tasks, leaving Miguel with time to provide greater value to his clients and to deepen his relationships with them. He had more time for his family, too.

11: DELEGATION LINK

How Your Delegation Link Interacts with Other Links

Here are examples of how this link interacts with the other eleven:

Boundary-setting: Holding staff accountable for their performance requires drawing a line between supervisor and direct-report.

Communication/Relationships: Leading and managing teams depends greatly on building positive relationships and communicating effectively.

Decision-making: Delegating begins with decisions: what to delegate, to whom, and so on.

Drive: Choosing how and what—even if—to delegate depends on your entire approach to work.

Goal-setting/Prioritization: Delegating effectively involves helping your direct-reports prioritize the work you assign them.

Health: Delegating more at work may free up time to spend in your personal life. Limitations on your health may induce you to delegate some tasks or responsibilities.

Organization of Objects/Data: Organizing your objects and data enables you to delegate more easily. When you are absent, others can do some of your tasks because they can find the necessary information, and so on.

Planning: Planning early enough enables you to delegate more effectively.

Reinvention: Resisting change or latching onto it deeply affects the people who report to you or try to help you.

Resources: Having someone to assist you is a valuable resource. You may also delegate to someone the responsibility of obtaining necessary resources, e.g., purchasing new equipment.

Task/Project Management: Having clarity about all your tasks and projects enables (and motivates) you to delegate.

Link 12 Drive

"I have such a drive that it's not an issue whether I will succeed. I will."
  —Karen, CEO, marketing supply company

Drive plays a crucial role in productivity. It supplies the psychic energy necessary for high achievement. Your Drive pushes your work forward, like driving a golf ball towards a hole. Psychic energy differs from the physical energy of the Health link (Chapter 14). You may have a strong drive to accomplish something, for example, but physical weakness won't let you.

This Link Propels You

Your Drive link propels you towards your work. It encompasses all the mental factors that influence how you approach a task. Do you attack it? Avoid it? Get it over with? Lose yourself in it? Your intensity of effort, motivation level, and attitude comprise your approach. They determine how much your Drive link energizes you.

"To drive" is to supply power for a thing.[6] Your drive is your personal power in applied action. That power sweeps you through your work—or creates a barrier against it—depending on your approach.

Components of the Drive Link that Affect Productivity

The Drive link has three main components. Consistently high productivity requires reliably strong effort, high motivation, and a positive, "can do" attitude.

12: DRIVE LINK

- **Effort:** Effort is the force, urgency, and focus you apply to a task. Your effort may wax or wane, depending on your motivation and attitude. Effort may not always be visible; it applies to intensity of thought, too, not just action.

- **Motivation:** Motivation is your desire to perform a task, the intention that inspires you to put forth the effort, and the reason you do it. Without a certain level of motivation, you cannot work. With great motivation, your work achieves new heights.

    "When you're really excited and passionate about something," notes Jing Song, an architect, "It's amazing how you find the time for it and the other things you need to do. You're energized." Depending on the situation and your attitude, your motivation may be extrinsic or intrinsic:

    > Enthusiasm is at the bottom of all progress! With it, there is accomplishment. Without it, there are only alibis.
    > — Henry Ford

    - **Extrinsic:** You do something because you want the rewards you will get when you succeed or you prefer to avoid the consequences you will get if you don't.

    - **Intrinsic:** You make a strong effort because that is who you are. Whether you enjoy the task or not, you do it to the best of your ability because that is your internal standard, your work ethic. Intrinsic motivation can be considered the more powerful because it falls fully within your control.

- **Attitude:** Attitude is your perspective about a task, person, or situation. It can also refer to a general view toward your world and life—such as optimism or pessimism. Your attitude can motivate or discourage you. It is the spirit you bring to your effort.

    Your attitude has a profound effect on your sense of power. Your viewpoint determines whether you "have to" or "choose to" do something: Same task, same goal, perhaps even same effort level—but a very different attitude.

    Feeling forced depresses energy; having choice boosts it. An attitude of choice also increases your peace of mind, freeing it from the resentment of "having to."

THE PRODUCTIVITY CHAIN

Effects of Drive on Productivity

When your Drive link is strong enough, it enhances your productivity because it empowers you to:

- **Focus on solutions.** A positive attitude empowers you to focus on solutions, not blame—a more productive approach that enhances your relationships with others. "I would much rather have somebody with a good attitude on my team, even if he lacks some skills or is not on the same level intellectually, than somebody with a negative attitude," asserts Betty, executive director of a not-for-profit.

- **Do what it takes.** When motivated to achieve your goals, you willingly do whatever it takes. As Alan, a sales consultant, explains, "Yesterday, I made twenty-five cold calls. Who does that? I get probably twenty rejections a day but I enjoy it. I've still got that determination to pick up additional business."

- **Work more quickly.** When you do your most important work with great intensity, you can accomplish much more in an hour than you normally could because your effort speeds you along.

- **Complete tasks without delay.** Your drive propels you towards task completion. A high level of motivation inspires you to begin and finish even those tasks that you find difficult, uncomfortable, or boring—however necessary they might be. You don't procrastinate; you initiate.

  A "get it done" attitude steers you past perfectionism—an approach to work that exemplifies lack of perspective. You must do certain tasks with complete accuracy and attention to detail, of course. Perfectionism, however, cannot distinguish those activities from the majority of tasks, whose quality standards vary from "superb" to "just good enough."

  > High motivation inspires you to begin and finish tasks you find difficult. You don't procrastinate, you initiate.

  As a result, perfectionism forces you to take much longer to complete tasks than necessary. A "get it done" attitude and sense of proportion, however, allow you to complete tasks as quickly as possible. What is "possible" depends on the tasks' importance, level of difficulty, and the consequences of errors.

12: DRIVE LINK

Walter's Drive Story

Walter joined a firm as lead researcher, with the promise of a research assistant once his workload reached a certain level. Within a year, he hit that level, but got no assistant. Over the next few years, he continued to exceed his targets without additional support.

It took a toll. Walter worked longer and longer hours, grew more resentful of his company, and eventually lost his girlfriend and his drive. That's when he hired me. "I was burned out," he admits. "I wanted a more balanced lifestyle but I couldn't see how it was possible."

Walter had thought getting more organized would help but quickly realized Organization of Objects/Data was just one of his weak links. After some weeks strengthening it and his Task Management link, "It just became clearer to me how much time I spent doing things an assistant could have done," he said.

When he calculated it, Walter determined that an assistant would free up at least 30 percent of his work week. Clearly, weak Delegation and Resources links contributed to his problem. His unbalanced Drive link, however, kept him from a solution.

> I focus on the bigger picture. I'm enjoying my life and my work a lot more now.
> Walter, lead researcher

Walter realized he had not actually pursued getting an assistant much, except to complain periodically. His attitude had been defeatist—he thought he would never get help, so he lacked motivation to push for it. When he did, he gave up easily and went back to work.

His work ethic was powerful and he applied enormous effort to everything he did. He worked so hard, it distracted him from the assistant problem for weeks at a time. "I would just do, do, do," he says. (See Chapter 23: *I Need to Work Harder* for more on this productivity myth.)

His negative attitude towards his company, meanwhile, had weakened his Communication/Relationships link—his manager and the supervisor of all the assistants had stopped taking him seriously. They knew they could put him off and he would accept it.

With some coaching, Walter began approaching his situation in a more powerful way. First, he stopped complaining to friends and coworkers about the promised assistant. It only soured his mood and darkened his view.

Second, he clarified exactly how the new assistant could help him. Focusing on the benefits motivated him to apply positive pressure on key decision-makers, and maintain that pressure through consistent follow-up. In a matter of weeks, he gained not only an assistant, but the respect of his colleagues.

"I can see now that I wasted so much time complaining and feeling bitter about the situation—much more than I spent actually trying to solve the problem," he says. "Today, keeping a positive attitude is job one," Walter continues. "I focus on the bigger picture. I'm enjoying my life and my work a lot more now. I'm starting to have fun again."

How to Strengthen Your Drive Link

If your Productivity Chain Analysis indicates you need to strengthen your Drive link, you might begin with these suggestions:

Challenge yourself to work diligently on tasks you dislike.

It's tempting to drag your feet on tasks you dislike. You may welcome distractions and reasons to avoid them. Challenge yourself to accomplish them as swiftly and accurately as possible. You might set a timer and race yourself.

You might also "bookend it" by contacting a trusted colleague when you begin and end the task. Knowing that someone expects to hear from you in an hour or two creates a sense of urgency, which is what disliked tasks need to speed them along.

Understand and leverage what motivates you.

Why do you do what you do? If you answer "to make a living," dig deeper: What is this living? What makes it worthwhile?

When you understand what motivates you, you can tap into the deep well of your personal power source. That energy enables you to accomplish more per hour than you would otherwise. You can also access it if or when your motivation starts to wane.

12: DRIVE LINK

Miguel, an account representative, used tasks he enjoyed as an incentive to do tasks he didn't. "I find something that juices me up during the day, that keeps me going, so I can do all these other things that are not so fun," he says.

> **TAKE ACTION**
> Write down why you do what you do and what lifestyle it serves. Dig deep to discover what motivates you.

Trust in abundance.

Fear of scarcity poisons productivity. When you think there aren't enough customers to go around, enough resources in the office, enough money for your needs, and so on, you become defensive, negative, and resentful. These attitudes are counterproductive.

When you trust in abundance, on the other hand, you are more open, sharing, willing to take risks, and philosophical about losses. If this attitude doesn't make you more productive, it will make you—and the people around you—happier.

Keep an attitude of gratitude.

Approach your work with a sense of thanksgiving and you will continually find more things to be grateful for. An attitude of gratitude helps you put a positive spin on any situation, and find peace of mind and acceptance when you need them most.

With a little creativity, gratitude can turn obstacles into opportunities. Gratitude works because it requires you to enlarge your perspective—to step back and see how this particular situation may prove useful or meaningful in the context of your whole life.

In the context of today, an attitude of gratitude can motivate you to work diligently and to connect your work with a higher purpose, such as helping others. That higher purpose may motivate you further.

THE PRODUCTIVITY CHAIN

How Your Drive Link Interacts with Other Links

Here are examples of how this link interacts with the other eleven:

Boundary-setting: Shutting down an inner perfectionist or procrastinator requires firm mental boundaries.

Communication/Relationships: Communicating your attitude to others is inevitable. Positive or negative, your attitude affects how people relate to you. Their attitudes influence your outlook and relationships with them, as well.

Decision-making: Changing your attitude or level of urgency towards a task requires a decision.

Delegation: Choosing how and what—even if—to delegate depends on your entire approach to work.

Goal-setting/Prioritization: Achieving your goals requires a high motivation level and can-do attitude. Inspiring goals, on the other hand, can motivate you.

Health: Maintaining sound physical, mental, and emotional health positively influences your attitude, motivation level, and effort level.

Organization of Objects/Data: Having an organized work space contributes to a sense of control, which creates a more positive attitude.

Planning: A clear plan motivates you to implement it. A mindset that respects the value of planning makes planning a bit easier.

Reinvention: Cultivating an attitude that embraces change enhances your ability to adapt to change.

Resources: Having sufficient resources contributes to a positive attitude. Self-awareness and self-knowledge enables you to better manage your motivation.

Task/Project Management: Viewing your task and project management system in a positive light contributes to its effectiveness because you are more likely to use it regularly, which is what makes it work.

Link

 **Goal-setting/ Prioritization**

"Just asking the questions has value: Why do I want to make more money? What do I really want? When I reflect on what makes me happy, what gives me energy, what I feel good about at the end of the day, the clarity just happens."
—Blythe, chief information officer

The Goal-setting/Prioritization link clarifies what you want to achieve, both big picture and small. While goal-setting and prioritization are distinct from each other, they are so interrelated that they share one link. Goal-setting articulates goals; prioritization puts them in order according to some standard.

Ranking your goals on different levels, including roles, projects, and tasks, enables you to decide how to spend your time on a daily basis. You achieve your productivity targets when all the links in your Productivity Chain cooperate to pull in the direction of your goals and priorities.

This Link Guides You

Your Goal-setting/Prioritization link guides you and your work, providing direction for all your decisions and actions. Your purpose, mission, vision, values, and needs—which inform your goals and priorities—act as your north star, guiding you to attain or maintain the life that best suits you.

When your actions align with your "true north," you access your personal power at its source deep within you.

> Goal-setting articulates goals; prioritization puts them in order according to some standard.

Components of Goal-setting that Affect Productivity

Goal-setting is a complex process, involving many components. It evolves over time. When your needs or circumstances change or you achieve a particular goal, the process begins anew. Contributing factors for your personal- and organization-centered goal-setting include:

- **Organizational Goals:** Your individual or departmental goals ideally align with those of the larger organization.
- **Objectives:** Your objectives are the smaller goals designed to help you achieve a larger goal.
- **Milestones:** Your milestones are the events or completions that mark your progress toward goal achievement.
- **Purpose:** Your purpose is your reason for doing and being. It answers why you work and live.
- **Mission:** Your mission describes what you do—the special contribution you make at work or in your life at large.
- **Vision:** Your vision is the picture of what you would like to ultimately achieve.
- **Values:** Your values are the principles and standards that matter to you and/or your organization.
- **Needs:** Your needs are what you must have in order to accomplish your mission, do your job, or be fulfilled.

Goal-setting affects your identity—both who you are now and who you want to be in the future. You become your future self by committing in the present to reach certain goals, such as getting a masters degree or practicing patience with a spouse.

Types of Prioritization that Affect Productivity

Prioritizing is actually a very specific kind of decision-making. Nevertheless, prioritization inhabits the Goal-setting link (rather than the Decision-making link) because effective prioritizing is impossible without goals.

13: GOAL-SETTING/PRIORITIZATION LINK

Prioritizing ranks your roles, projects, and tasks in order of importance and urgency or another criteria, depending on your goals. It holds your action options against the standard of the goals you want to reach, the vision you want to achieve, the person you want to be. Ideally, this comparison helps you decide what to keep, discard, or transform.

> *Things which matter most must never be at the mercy of things which matter least.*
> Johann Wolfgang von Goethe

Prioritizing occurs on a number of levels:

- **Roles:** You may prioritize the roles you play at different times in your life. You might focus on work—rather than romance—early in your career, for instance. You may wait until your children grow before running for public office. Or you may put your role as rainmaker in your organization before your role as manager.
- **Projects:** Prioritizing projects might require completely letting go of some projects, clients, or prospects that do not align with your goals. Although they may have personal, sentimental, financial, or other value to you, they only siphon time and energy from your goals. You may send other projects to the back burner to await more active attention in the future.
- **Tasks:** Prioritizing tasks enables you to decide what to do this minute, this day, this week, and so on. It empowers you, for example, to choose working on a report over updating your Facebook status "real quick."

Effects of Goal-setting/Prioritization on Productivity

Regularly evaluating what matters most—and ranking your tasks, projects, and roles accordingly—brings meaning to your work and your life. When your Goal-setting/Prioritization link is strong enough, it empowers you to:

- **Accomplish what you want.** You are more likely to achieve the results you want when you clarify them and take action. Research on resolutions indicates that the very act of setting goals increases the likelihood of achieving them.[7] Referring to them regularly keeps you on track.

"What is the highest and best use of my time?" asks David, an executive recruiter. "It's to be in front of people." His schedule and call list reflect that priority. So do his substantial commissions. He keeps his goals uppermost in his mind each day and it pays off.

- **Spend your time more wisely.** Clear goals and priorities enable you to quickly embrace commitments, objects, and information that align with them, and let go of—or don't take on—those that do not. When you rely on them, your goals and priorities clear the clutter from your schedule, mind, and office, enabling you to perform more productively.

    As RJ, a management consultant, explains, setting goals and priorities saves time and money. "When planning a vacation, you decide where you're going and how long you'll be there. You work back from that. Otherwise, you buy new golf gear and end up on a cruise."

- **Feel a greater sense of control.** Effective, consistent, goal-aligned prioritizing allows you to set your own agenda. Many people "prioritize" by responding to whatever is loudest—the new email, the call, the comment of a supervisor. This method leaves them feeling at the mercy of others and usually overwhelmed. Or they don't prioritize at all. In that case, when everything is equally important, nothing is important.

    Prioritizing every morning and again throughout the day puts you in charge. It's like checking in with your stomach and looking at what is already on your plate before you go back to the all-you-can-eat buffet.

- **Motivate others to accomplish more.** When you set goals for yourself, your staff, and perhaps your entire organization, you have the opportunity to increase everyone's productivity by making those goals as wise, growth-inducing, and inspiring as possible.

    Setting a goal to increase sales by 30 percent (if that is attainable), for example, is more inspiring and productivity-inducing than setting it for a more modest five percent.

13: GOAL-SETTING/PRIORITIZATION LINK

Linda's Goal-setting/Prioritization Story

Linda had founded a website design firm a few years ago and her vision was clear. She wanted high-quality in every area: websites, client relationships, employee relationships, and revenues.

On the ground level, however, her perspective clouded. Everything related to her business, so "it all seemed important," she says. She had a master list of tasks and identified what she wanted to accomplish each day. But by mid-morning, her priorities usually took a back seat to whatever problems or opportunities arose. She felt out of control and didn't see how the business could keep growing if she could barely manage it now.

As an exercise, Linda reviewed the ten tasks she had assigned herself that day and estimated how long each would take. Then she checked her calendar. She had four hours reserved for meetings, plus lunch with one of her designers. She also needed to check email and be available for her staff. Then she had to rush to her kids' school. That left her two hours of "free" time.

> Linda's prioritizing had been wish-list making.

Linda realized she was trying to fit seven hours of work into a two-hour slot. It was an epiphany. Linda's prioritizing had been wish-list making. No wonder she failed each day to accomplish what she wanted. Her "today" tasks reflected what was important to her but didn't take her available time into account.

Armed with both her task list and calendar, Linda learned to prioritize more realistically. She considered not just how important a task was, but how long it would take. In this way, she used her Planning link skills to support her Goal-setting/Prioritization link.

It took some time but, gradually, realistic prioritizing became a strong skill for Linda. On the rare occasion when she overbooked herself, she quickly realized the cause and got back on track.

How to Strengthen Your Goal-setting/Prioritization Link

If your Productivity Chain Analysis indicates you need to strengthen your Goal-setting/Prioritization link, you might begin with these suggestions:

Define your personal and professional "true north."

Take time to contemplate what matters to you and what you want your life and work to mean. Clarifying your mission, vision, purpose, values, and needs guides you in this process.

Defining your "true north" *is* a process. Even if you take yourself on a weekend retreat to write it all out, the answers will continue to unfold over time. Nevertheless, living in accordance with your "true north"—whatever it is at the present time—enhances your sense of integrity and efficacy.

Make your goals SMARTT.

Make sure your goals are SMARTT, my variation of the popular acronym, SMART. In this version, "relevant" replaces "realistic" and "tough" has been added. SMARTT goals meet the following six criteria:

Specific—clear and well-defined;
Measurable—objectively measurable, at least at start and end;
Attainable—humanly possible in the time allowed;
Relevant—to your purpose and your organization's mission;
Time-oriented—having a well-defined start and end date/time;
Tough—challenging and inspiring, testing your skills and will.

Setting a traditional SMART goal transforms a wish or desire into an actionable plan. When you add the final "T," however, you leverage your motivation. Research has found that mediocre goals inspire mediocre effort.[8]

> *A goal without a plan is just a wish.*
> Antoine de Saint-Exupery

Challenging goals, on the other hand, motivate you to rise to the challenge. SMARTT goals spark your enthusiasm, pulling you from where you are to where you want to be.

Schedule due dates sparingly.

You may be tempted to assign fake due-dates to new tasks so you can prioritize them easily. Don't. These "aspirational" deadlines usually backfire, adding to your sense of being barraged rather than helping you sift through the clutter.

13: GOAL-SETTING/PRIORITIZATION LINK

You end up "snoozing" your "priority" reminders or dismissing them altogether. And, since everything has a due date, you can't tell which are real. Instead, set due dates sparingly and prioritize by reviewing all your task options using a practice such as one of those described below.

Commit to a prioritization practice.

You can prioritize in many different ways. What matters most is that you make prioritizing a daily practice for tasks, and a slightly less frequent practice for projects.

> When everything is equally important, nothing is important.

Here are several common prioritizing strategies. You could "audition" them until you find the one you like.

- **Job Goals:** Use your performance goals as your guide. Do whatever advances these goals first and anything "extracurricular" later.

- ***7 Habits* Time Matrix:** Dr. Stephen Covey recommends categorizing tasks and projects by quadrant.[9] Quadrant I activities are urgent and important. Quadrant II's are important but not urgent. Quadrant III's are urgent but unimportant, and Quadrant IV's are neither urgent nor important.

    Prioritize by putting Quadrant II and I activities first (in that order), and do as little of the rest as possible. To learn more, read his book, *The 7 Habits of Highly Effective People*.

- **Allen Method:** In *Getting Things Done*, David Allen advises considering your context (setting and tools) first; then your schedule to see how much time you have; then your energy level; and then—all things being equal—the goal-based importance of a given task.[10]

- **Frog First:** Brian Tracy recommends doing your most important, difficult, and/or loathsome task first thing in the morning in his book, *Eat That Frog!*[11] It energizes your day.

- **Bottom Line:** In *Never Check E-Mail in the Morning*, Julie Morgenstern advocates using dollars as your prioritizing standard.[12] The more an action contributes to the bottom line, the higher its priority.

THE PRODUCTIVITY CHAIN

How Your Goal-setting/Prioritization Link Interacts with Other Links

Here are examples of how this link interacts with the other eleven:

Boundary-setting: Knowing your goals, values, and priorities helps you say "no" or "not now" to the people, interruptions, opportunities, and distractions that might interfere with achieving those goals, and so on.

Communication/Relationships: Inspiring others to help you achieve your (and your organization's) goals requires persuasive communication and influence in the relationships.

Decision-making: Goal-setting requires deciding what is important and when. Prioritization is a specific kind of decision-making.

Delegation: Delegating effectively involves helping your direct-reports prioritize the work you assign them.

Drive: Achieving your goals requires a high motivation level and can-do attitude. Inspiring goals, on the other hand, can motivate you.

Health: Maintaining your health requires knowing what matters to you and setting goals to achieve it. Health must be a top priority for high productivity to be sustained.

Organization of Objects/Data: Clarifying your goals and values enables you to more quickly decide whether to keep or delete objects and data.

Planning: Planning carves out the time to do the work to achieve goals. The limited hours in a day induce you to prioritize.

Reinvention: Changing circumstances inspire you to adapt your priorities accordingly.

Resources: Continuing your professional education or obtaining a certain tool begins with setting that goal and then making it a priority.

Task/Project Management: Collecting your tasks and projects in one system enables you to prioritize them effectively—which includes matching your priorities with your larger goals.

Link

 **14 Health**

"You need to take care of yourself because if you're sick, you're worthless to everybody else."
—Reeza, manager, accounting firm

The Health link forms the foundation of your productivity. It represents the physical spring from which your thoughts and actions flow. It is the ***being*** link that balances all the ***doing*** links.

Unlike most of the others, the Health link includes some factors beyond your control, such as age, disease, or disability. Still, you do have power over how you handle those factors and your self-care.

This Link Energizes You

Your Health link energizes you so you can work—and play—at sustainably high levels. The energy's sources are physical, mental, emotional, spiritual, and social. That energy is the power inside that enables you to exert power in the outside world and be productive there.

The Health link's physical energy differs from the psychic energy of the Drive link (see Chapter 12), although—as with all links—the two do overlap. You can be bursting with physical energy, for example, but if you have no motivation to produce, you might use that energy to work on some low-value activity.

Components of Health that Affect Productivity

Your Health link encompasses a number of components:
- **Physical Health:** Your work performance expands or contracts depending on your body's limits. Physical variables that affect productivity include your physical fitness; diet; quantity and

quality of sleep; and presence of illness, disease, or disability.

- **Mental Health:** As an organ, your brain is part of your physical body. How your brain functions determines your mental health. Mental factors that deserve special consideration include addictions and brain-based conditions, such as depression. (See Appendix C: *Productivity-Related Terms* for more about these factors.)

- **Emotional Health:** Emotions affect your whole body. Grief and infatuation, for example, can impair concentration and motivation. How well you manage and process your emotions—at work and home—affects your productivity.

- **Spiritual Health:** Most people seek connection with something greater than themselves. It may be nature, knowledge, religion, family, principles, or college football. Certain practices, such as helping others, having a sense of wonder, or following a moral code, contribute to this connection. Whatever your spiritual path, following it can add meaning to your work and life. For some, it provides access to inner strength and guidance, too.

- **Social Health:** Your social support system, including family and friends, affects (and reflects) your overall health. Greater social support correlates with greater well-being. This aspect of the Health link overlaps with the Communication/Relationships link. It serves here as a reminder that positive relationships matter for their own sake and for you personally, not just to help get things done.

Balancing Acts

"After the kids went to bed, I used to be on the laptop, banging out some emails. Now I can be more 'present' at home."
—Brody, vice president of sales

Everyone benefits from balancing work and play, effort and rest, difficulty and ease. Recharging your batteries makes you more productive. Some ideas about balance to consider:

- **Balance is a practice, not a permanent state.** You may think of "balance" as some equilibrium you can finally achieve. In reality, balancing is a lifelong process of adjustments as you swing from one imbalance to another.

It's like walking. Stepping with your right leg, you're temporarily off balance. You don't fall (usually) because you shift momentum to the left leg quickly—one force counteracts the other. While you move, balancing is easy—you swing from one imbalanced state to another. If you kept one leg raised, however, you would eventually collapse with the strain.

Balancing your work and your personal life happens the same way—through a series of small, counteracting adjustments and course corrections. You work hard during the week and take the weekend off, for instance. Too many late nights? You heed your distress signals—better known as "stress"—and swing the pendulum towards sleep.

Tessa practiced balance after opening her own store. "After I left my job to form my own business," she says, "I found myself really lonely. I missed that daily interaction. I started calling people to go to lunch with me. I found myself lacking energy, so I started going to the gym." Tessa listened to her stress and adjusted accordingly.

- **You balance the Three O's: Ourselves, Others, and Obligations.** Your pendulum actually goes in three directions, encouraging you to spend time in each of the Three O's. They are: *Ourselves*, meaning you and your health in every sense; *Others*, including your romantic partner, family, friends, and pets; and *Obligations*, including those at work, at home, and in your community.

- **You can't cram it all into one day or week.** This type of "balancing," made popular in the media, generates stress. Instead, think in terms of a month, a year, maybe even seasons of your life. During a given period, you may emphasize different O's to a greater or lesser extent.

Effects of Health on Productivity

Because it provides the energy they need to function, your Health link's impact on other links is quick and profound. A little weakness soon hurts them. A little extra strength, on the other hand, strengthens them, too. When your Health link is strong enough, you:

- **Sustain your energy.** Taking care of your physical body generates energy. It enhances your ability to concentrate and apply effort to your actions. "I go to the gym three times a week," notes Daniel, a training and development VP. "It gives me energy, strength, stamina. I feel better at sixty-three than I did at fifty." All of my most productive clients exercise regularly.
- **Improve your perspective.** Taking time off puts work into perspective. It enables you to remember why you work in the first place and refreshes your view about work-related problems.
- **Attract others.** Taking care of yourself, which may include treating any illness you have, demonstrates competence and responsibility. Other people want to spend time with you when you aren't a bundle of unmet needs or misdirected emotions. "People can tell when you feel good," adds Zach. "They definitely can tell when you don't!"
- **Build support.** Your support network and self-care enable you to meet challenges and difficulties with resilience and strength. You move through problems without getting immobilized by them.

Austin's Health Story

Austin had achieved a great deal of success as owner of a chain of discount stores. Materially, he had everything he wanted, but he felt too exhausted and consumed by work to enjoy it. He consulted several experts to help him turn his life around.

First, a specialist's evaluation determined that he had Attention Deficit Disorder (ADD), as he had long suspected. The diagnosis helped him understand difficulties he had experienced in school and since, despite his intelligence. As the doctor explained, it was as if Austin ran around the same track as other people, only his shoes were encased in invisible concrete blocks. He needed more time and effort to reach the same goal.

14: HEALTH LINK

The more he learned about ADD, the more Austin realized the importance of self-care. Anything that improved concentration and focus helped minimize the negative effects of ADD. "I started looking at life from a different perspective," he says, "sleeping properly, eating properly, not insulting myself with chemicals or fatigue or other things. That different perspective makes it easier for me to determine what has to be done and then get it done."

Already a marathon runner, Austin hired a registered dietician to develop a food plan to better fuel his body. "Once I got my nutrition in line," he continues, "it improved my ability to have and sustain energy throughout the day.

"I wasn't crashing in the afternoon anymore, my thinking was clearer, my moods—and how I treated people—improved. I stopped getting short with people. I solved problems calmly, without overreacting. That's something I do every day in my business, so I've got to be level-headed, even, and clear-minded."

> *"I wasn't crashing in the afternoon, my thinking was clearer, my moods—and how I treated people—improved.*
> Austin, owner, store chain

Next, productivity coaching helped Austin accomplish more in less time, freeing hours for his family. "When I come home now," he notes, "I spend time with my wife and kids. Before, I ate dinner, then went back to the office. When I improved my productivity, I cut most of that out."

Austin likes his life today. "I'm more relaxed now. In the past, my work clock never stopped. When I did sit on the couch for five minutes, I'd fall asleep because I was exhausted. Now I quit at a decent hour. My wife and I have a date one night a week, and so I cut out early then. I find it easier to turn the work switch off so I can enjoy my personal life."

How to Strengthen Your Health Link

If your Productivity Chain Analysis indicates you need to strengthen your Health link, begin immediately. When just beginning coaching, some clients say they don't feel they "deserve" to take time for Health—especially balance—until **after** they solve their productivity problem. They may feel bad about not exercising or eating healthily enough, but they also feel guilty for taking time

THE PRODUCTIVITY CHAIN

to go to the gym, enjoy a really good meal, or even have fun.

They don't realize that their Health (physical, mental, emotional, spiritual, and social) is just as important as the other links in their Productivity Chain. Soon, though, they understand that they need to address their Health link *first* so they have energy to achieve their other productivity goals.

If you feel guilty, as they did, please give yourself permission to take care of your health today. Still unconvinced? Read about the "I can't play until my work is done" myth (Chapter 27.)

To actually strengthen your Health link, you might begin with these suggestions:

Exercise, sleep, and eat well.

The effects on productivity of regular exercise, sufficient sleep, and a nutritionally-sound diet have been well proven and widely publicized. Exercise, sleep, and good food are especially important when other factors, such as a chronic illness, put your Health link at risk.

> Better keep yourself clean and bright; you are the window through which you must see the world.
> — George Bernard Shaw

"I'm so much more productive on the days when I've eaten well and done some kind of physical activity," declares Rachel, a director of foreign affairs. "I'm more focused. I have more confidence because I feel good."

Something is better than nothing when it comes to improving your physical health. Let go of thinking exercise "doesn't count" unless you have a heart rate of 160 for two hours (or whatever your "standard" is). Walking for twenty minutes counts, especially if you have not walked in months. Even catnaps help when you are sleep-deprived. And replacing your candy bar with a handful of raw walnuts makes a difference to your blood sugar levels today.

Apply the Four Pillars of Balance.

As previously noted, "balance" really means heeding your stress and taking action to counteract it. The faster your response, the greater your balance. Use the Four Pillars to guide your response at any moment.

1. **Be Aware.** Listen to your thoughts, feelings, and body so you can hear any stress. You might notice your stomach gurgling

with hunger. You might snap at your spouse or have difficulty falling asleep. Once you become aware of your stress, take action to ease it.

2. **Be Humble.** Admit that you can't do everything. Then reevaluate what you have already planned and set more realistic self-expectations going forward. (See Chapter 21: *I Can Do It All* for more about this exhausting productivity myth.)

3. **Be Simple.** Clear the existing clutter from your space, mind, and schedule. What activities, for example, can you let go of, reschedule, or do faster (i.e., less "perfectly") **today**? Simplicity enhances balance.

4. **Be First.** Take care of yourself first. Only then can you care for others. Only then can you be productive in a way you can sustain long term.

Disconnect from work completely sometimes.

Do no job-related work at least one day a week. Step away from your phone after a certain time each night. Unless you disengage periodically, you risk burnout.

Elite athletes take their rest time seriously; so should you. Disconnecting gives you the opportunity to recharge your batteries. It gives you a new perspective on your problems. It also boosts your sense of personal power when you know you can turn off work for a time.

> Taking time off puts work into perspective.

Leverage your energy.

Your physical energy fuels your productivity engine. To leverage it most effectively, don't try to maintain the same effort and focus for eight hours straight. Instead, alternate activities that require deep concentration with more mundane tasks.

Punctuate your day with short breaks by getting up, moving around, and changing your scenery. These "rests" renew your energy and help you get more done. "It's interval training for your work," says Melissa, my editor. And it's just as effective in the office as on the track.

THE PRODUCTIVITY CHAIN

Your natural rhythms influence your energy levels, too. Save your most challenging work for your brain's "power hours," whether morning, mid-day, or late evenings.

"I shoved my whole day forward by a couple of hours to play into my strength—morning time," says Joshua, CEO of a manufacturing firm. "It created dinner-with-the-family time. Now I get the best of both worlds. I'm at work when I'm most productive there, and I'm at home for the most productive family time."

14: HEALTH LINK

How Your Health Link Interacts with Other Links

Here are examples of how this link interacts with the other eleven:

Boundary-setting: Setting limits with yourself (to take a break or leave work, for instance) enables you to manage your energy and maintain your health.

Communication/Relationships: Developing a network of family, friends, and/or compatible people increases your social health, which may translate into better mental and physical health. Communicating clearly with medical professionals can benefit your health, as well.

Decision-making: Taking care of your health and balancing your activities requires making decisions every day, many times a day.

Delegation: Delegating more at work may free up time to spend in your personal life. Limitations on your health may induce you to delegate some tasks or responsibilities.

Drive: Maintaining sound physical, mental, and emotional health positively influences your attitude, motivation level, and effort level.

Goal-setting/Prioritization: Maintaining your health requires knowing what matters to you and setting goals to achieve it. Health must be a top priority for high productivity to be sustained.

Organization of Objects/Data: Having certain brain-based conditions, such as Attention Deficit Disorder, makes organizing more difficult. Disorganization can be stress-inducing for some people, and clutter can cause injury, e.g., twisting an ankle on stacks of files on the floor.

Planning: Planning enables you to earmark time to take care of your health, e.g., to exercise, so other activities don't interfere.

Reinvention: Changing mental and physical health creates an opportunity to practice being adaptable and flexible.

Resources: Maintaining your health requires you to tap into resources, such as physicians, nutritional information, and classes (e.g., yoga or kickboxing). It also draws on your own self-knowledge regarding preferences, and so on.

Task/Project Management: Losing weight, training for a race, or staying fit are all projects for you to manage. An effective task and project management system, meanwhile, helps you work more effectively and sleep more soundly.

Link 15
Organization
of Objects/Data

"It feels good to know where to get something, rather than ripping through files or getting all antsy and aggravated about it. I don't think I knew until I started working with a productivity coach how much I disliked clutter."
—Amanda, director, human resources

Organization of Objects/Data refers to the physical arrangement of your work space and its contents. It is a means to an end. The "end" might be quickly executing tasks. It might be the ease of locating a document without rifling through a mountain of "stuff" first. Or it might be the pleasure of seeing a favorite art piece displayed on a clear desktop.

This Link Economizes Your Work

Your Organization of Objects/Data link economizes your work by enabling you to access needed information and things without wasted time or effort. Keeping just enough order to maintain efficiency increases your sense of personal power and self-control. Since clutter stifles energy, organizing your objects and data lets your energy flow freely.

Giving "Organization" New Meaning

The Productivity Chain's conceptualization of organization is far narrower and more concrete than what most people mean when they exclaim, "I just need to get more organized!" This book's premise, described in the first few chapters, is that "getting organized" won't solve most people's productivity problems because Organization of Objects/Data is just one of twelve links in

15: ORGANIZATION OF OBJECTS/DATA LINK

> **TAKE ACTION: Are You Sure You Need to Get Organized?**
>
> If you just opened this book, the question above is for you. You may think that you need to "get organized" to perform more effectively. In reality, organization is just one of twelve factors that determine how productive you can be—just one link in your Productivity Chain.
>
> To make the best use of your time and energy—and avoid wasting either—don't implement the suggestions listed in this chapter until you take these steps:
>
> 1. Read Chapter 1: *A New Productivity Model* to understand the Productivity Chain. If you're not convinced, read Chapter 24: *I Need to Get More Organized* (in Section III: *Productivity Myths*).
> 2. Read "When Are You Organizing 'Just Enough'—or 'Too Much?'" in this chapter (box).
> 3. Analyze your own Productivity Chain (Chapter 4: *Identify Solutions*).

the Chain. Those other links contribute just as much to your performance level. If they are quite weak, their impact may be felt even more.

Unless your Organization of Objects/Data link is so weak that it undermines your stronger links, then "getting more organized" won't make you significantly more productive. You might temporarily feel better, but you waste your time—the exact opposite of what you want.

Your Organization of Objects/Data link may, of course, legitimately need some shoring up. If so, this chapter offers some suggestions to help you do just that. It also explains more about the link so you can better decide just how strong yours is.

What Are "Objects" and "Data?"

While the Productivity Chain model defines "organization" quite narrowly, it makes the definitions of "objects" and "data" fairly broad.

- **Objects:** Objects are anything physical, including knickknacks, pens, marketing flyers, and so on. But it applies to much more than items you can hold in your hand. Objects include office furniture and shelving, equipment such as printers, papers, manila folders, books, personal belongings, gadgets, and so on.

- **Data:** Data means information, which is intangible. Information includes facts, figures, and ideas. When organized, information can be translated into useful knowledge and/or action. Data takes many forms. It might be on paper or digital, such as emails or electronic files of all types.

Sometimes organizing involves determining the best, most accessible, format for your information. It may make sense to put someone's contact information in your database, rather than keep the business card, for example.

Effects of Organization of Objects/Data on Productivity

When your Organization of Objects/Data link is strong enough, it enhances your productivity in a number of ways. It enables you to:

- **Be creative.** Letting go of clutter often results in a flood of new ideas and possibilities. Why? There is space for them. Sounds metaphysical, but it is a practical reality.
- **Spend time profitably.** You do your work, rather than waste time:
  - finding a clear place to do your work;
  - looking for things so you can do your work;
  - re-purchasing items you can't find;
  - re-doing your work because you can't find what you already did;
  - feeling trapped and frustrated by all the things that interfere with your work.
- **Respond nimbly to the unexpected.** You might fear that being organized will make you rigid, but you actually become more flexible. You can more easily seize opportunities when you can find what you need almost instantly.
- **Improve others' productivity.** People have a clear place to leave work for you—on your desk, for instance, instead of on your

15: ORGANIZATION OF OBJECTS/DATA LINK

Exercise: When Are You Organizing "Just Enough"—or "Too Much?"

Too much time spent organizing is counterproductive. To determine whether you are organizing "just enough" or "too much," see which category below fits you best.

"Just Enough"
- You quickly find what you need to do your work.
- You have enough order so you have room to work.
- You don't waste time hunting for, or replacing, information or things.
- You can usually maintain this order in just minutes a day.

Your Organization of Objects/Data link is strong enough.

"Too Much"
You might spend too much time organizing for different reasons:

A. You don't know how to organize.
- You aren't good at sorting or categorizing.
- You don't know where to put things or where to find them.
- You may have struggled with organizing objects or data for years.

Your Organization of Objects/Data link needs to be strengthened. You may benefit from working with a Professional Organizer.

B. You delay doing your work.
If deadlines approach and your organizing does **nothing** to help you meet them, it's too much. Organizing should be a servant to the master of your priorities. When it dominates, you procrastinate. Stop organizing and start producing!

Your Organization of Objects/Data link is strong enough. Your Drive and Goal-setting/Prioritization links may be weak.

C. You try to fix problems that "organizing" can't repair.
You never feel organized "enough" because you're trying to use it to solve some other problem. Organizing can't keep you from taking on too many responsibilities, communicating poorly, avoiding decisions, delegating irresponsibly, feeling unmotivated, not prioritizing, etc.

Your Organization of Objects/Data link is probably strong enough. Do a Productivity Chain Analysis to learn which links can solve your real problem. Then take positive, corrective action.

empty chair. They may get quicker responses from you because their requests aren't lost in the clutter.

"Organized enough" shared spaces help everyone work more efficiently. Jenna, a director of research and development, recently spearheaded the effort to organize her department's lab. "Getting organized takes the mental burden off," she says.

"Knowing what we have and accessing it easily—and therefore keeping it relevant, current, and useful—helps us tremendously. We have multiple people in that lab and they need to be able to spot things quickly."

Laura's "Just Enough" Organization Story

Laura, a sales representative for a pharmaceutical firm, had a simple, elegant, and highly effective filing method she called her "Oh, shoot" system. It exemplifies a "strong enough" Organization of Objects/Data link.

Her company's software program managed her quotes and orders but didn't store the quotes in a readily-accessible way, so Laura kept a paper record of these in case a problem arose later.

She could have made a folder for each client or each quote, which would have been "organized." Since she rarely had problems, however, that effort seemed time-consuming and wasteful. Instead, she put the quote printouts in a tray on a shelf near her desk.

When someone did raise a concern, Laura would think "Oh, shoot! I need that record." Since she always added to the top of the pile, it was sorted chronologically. She could quickly skip to the approximate location in the stack, sift through some dated, ordered papers, and find the one she needed.

> *Good order is the foundation of all things.*
> Edmund Burke

A couple of times a year, she would toss the bottom half of the pile. If no problems had arisen by then, none would.

In recent years, Laura's "Oh, shoot" system has gone digital. She saves the quotes as PDFs in one big folder. It has still kept her organized "just enough."

15: ORGANIZATION OF OBJECTS/DATA LINK

How to Strengthen Your Organization of Objects/Data Link

If your Productivity Chain Analysis reveals that Organization of Objects/Data really *is* a weak link of yours, making it strong enough so it doesn't undermine your other links will improve your productivity. (See Chapter 4: *Identify Solutions* for more about that analysis.) Here are some suggestions:

Separate "organized" from "neat."

Organizing makes things neater, but making things neater does not make them organized. If you straighten your office and it falls apart again in a couple of days, it might be that you got it neat, not organized.

Organizing your objects and data ensures that everything has a place designed with purpose and practical maintenance in mind, and that you have a system for keeping it that way.

To strengthen your Organization of Objects/Data link, think about how you will **maintain** the order as you create it. If you want to put an item neatly in a box, for example, consider how easily you could get things into and out of that box going forward, and exactly where to keep the box. When you truly get organized, neatness takes care of itself.

Listen to your "laziness."

For many people, "laziness" is really an internal efficiency wizard. It wants you to use minimal effort to accomplish tasks, so it inspires you to store items according to frequency of use.

- **Daily:** Keep within arm's reach the physical items you use daily—no bending, stretching, lifting, or opening required. Do it digitally by marking files and folders as "Favorites."
- **Frequently:** Use standing files on your desktop for "hot" paper files. Create "Shortcuts" to quickly access your "hot" electronic files.
- **Rarely:** Put things you must keep but rarely access (e.g., tax records) as far away as you like. It might be off-site, across the room, or in a drawer that you have to kneel down to open.

Another "lazy" strategy: Pretend it's a year from now and you want a certain file, piece of information, or object. Where would you look for it first? The place that comes to mind is the place to keep it now.

Listening to your "laziness" helps you let go of old ideas about where you "should" keep your personnel files or expense reports, and so on. There are no "shoulds" in organizing except one: your strategies "should" meet your needs. Even the ideas in this book are only suggestions.

Simplify your filing to speed retrieval.

When creating a file system, either paper or digital, keep it simple. You will never use the vast majority of what you file—including the resource folders containing all those great articles and notes. There is no value, then, in getting fancy with your filing.

Having fewer folders speeds filing and retrieval. It takes less time to sift through the contents of one large folder than to sort through many thinner folders, trying to remember how you categorized things. Advances in computer search tools make filing and retrieval even faster. You might, for example, put your saved emails in just two folders: Keep for Sure and Just in Case.

Remember this simple principle: The time you spend creating and maintaining your files should be less than the time you spend using their contents.

Switch your default setting to "delete."

Many people suffer from what I call "material constipation." The U.S. consumer culture values excess. We "consume" vast quantities of paper, information, and things. And what we get, we keep. When we keep too much, it becomes clutter. In any form—physical, digital, or mental—clutter gets in the way.

To unclog the system and get your productivity energy flowing again, switch your internal default setting from "keep" to "delete." To change your default, change your questions. The "keep" mindset asks, "What if I might need this someday?" The "delete" mindset asks "What is the worst possible thing that could happen if I did not have this information?"[13]

This pertinent question, which applies to objects, too, comes

15: ORGANIZATION OF OBJECTS/DATA LINK

from Barbara Hemphill's *Taming the Paper Tiger*. It begins with deletion in mind. (In most cases, the "worst possible thing" is not dire.)

With your "delete" default in place, you can address clutter at both ends of the process.

1. **Limit your intake.** As new emails, documents, and physical objects come into your world, assume they will go in the trash immediately or soon. Keep only the exceptional items that prove their worth.

2. **Let go of excess.** Go through your existing piles and files and let go of all that you can. Begin reviewing the items you use currently so the clearing can immediately affect your productivity. Pack the old stuff in boxes to address (or toss) later.

> **TAKE ACTION**
> Ask yourself Barbara Hemphill's question: "What is the worst possible thing that could happen if I did not have this information?"

As you simplify—letting go of clutter—you discover a truth: The less you have, the more easily you see what really matters.

THE PRODUCTIVITY CHAIN

How Your Organization of Objects/Data Link Interacts with Other Links

Here are examples of how this link interacts with the other eleven:

Boundary-setting: Discarding an object, paper, or email means saying "no" and committing to that limit.

Communication/Relationships: Organizing your work area makes you feel more comfortable with inviting others in. It makes others confident that they can communicate by leaving notes without fear they will be lost.

Decision-making: Organizing requires you to decide what to keep, what to toss, where to keep your objects and data, and for how long.

Delegation: Organizing your objects and data enables you to delegate more easily. When you are absent, others can do some of your tasks because they can find the necessary information, and so on.

Drive: Having an organized work space contributes to a sense of control, which creates a more positive attitude.

Goal-setting/Prioritization: Clarifying your goals and values enables you to more quickly decide whether to keep or delete objects and data.

Health: Having certain brain-based conditions, such as Attention Deficit Disorder, makes organizing more difficult. Disorganization can be stress-inducing for some people, and clutter can cause injury, e.g., twisting an ankle on stacks of files on the floor.

Planning: Being organized facilitates planning projects and events because it makes materials and information accessible.

Reinvention: Keeping your objects and data organized requires constant adaptation to changing circumstances. "Hot" files, for example, cool quickly, to be replaced by newer projects.

Resources: Being organized, especially when it involves liberal use of the trash can, saves on storage costs and replacement costs of resources. It facilitates professional development by making reference files accessible.

Task/Project Management: Organizing objects and data often occurs in conjunction with creating task and project lists. A paper can be tossed or filed once the relevant action goes on a list.

Link

 **16 Planning**

"I have completely cleared the clutter from my schedule."
—Delaney, tax and estate attorney

While "busy" people prefer to jump in and do, productive people plan first. As a result, they spend their time more effectively and efficiently, minimizing waste. That shrewd approach to time is the function of the Planning link. The link encompasses all kinds of planning, including one of the most crucial: scheduling.

This Link Operationalizes Your Work

Your Planning link operationalizes your work, preparing it for action. That preparation includes scheduling, which allocates time for specific activities. Your calendar is where wishes meet the reality of time. Planning greatly enhances your personal power by giving you greater control over your schedule and your expectations.

Types of Planning

There are many kinds of planning; the following are particularly relevant to productivity:

- **Breaking down projects.** Projects can be big or small, but they always require multiple steps—called tasks—to complete. In order to move into action, you have to break your project into its component tasks. This is project planning.

    Your plan might involve complex charts and scores of people, or it might be a sticky note only you see. Either way, it specifies what tasks need to happen, when, and by whom. (See the box on the next page for details.)

THE PRODUCTIVITY CHAIN

> **Project Planning: Chopping Up Your Pineapples**
>
> Fruit can teach us a lot about planning our work. Imagine you are a hungry, hurried fruit lover. You rush into the kitchen on your way out the door.
>
> **Scenario One:** You see a banana and a pineapple, both in their natural packaging. Which do you choose? The banana, of course. It's ready to eat.
>
> **Scenario Two:** You see a banana and a cup of pineapple chunks with a fork. Both options are equally ready to eat. Which do you choose? Now, it depends. Maybe you prefer one over the other. Maybe you need the nutrients that one possesses. Because they're both bite-sized, you can base your decision on relevant factors, rather than expediency.
>
> **The Analogy Breakdown**
>
> In this analogy, a single serving of fruit is a task. Some tasks are like bananas—easy, plentiful, and cheap. A low-priority email reply, for example. Other tasks are like the pineapple cup. They relate to something bigger, challenging, and valuable—the spiny pineapple project, which requires several actions to prepare.
>
> Project planning—chopping up the pineapple—enables your project tasks to "compete" with other tasks, rather than remain "hidden" under a thick skin. You can then prioritize all your tasks by their merit, rather than how easy they are to do. Project planning makes you more productive because it keeps you from eating a bunch of low-quality bananas while your valuable pineapples rot.

- **Scheduling activities.** Scheduling is your plan for when you will do a particular task. It requires setting an appointment on your calendar. It is one thing to set a goal and even break it down into steps. It is quite another to make time in your busy day for the work. Scheduling, then, is where intention becomes commitment—or not.

> Scheduling is where intention becomes commitment.

To be useful, your plan must be realistic. As you look at your calendar, estimate how long activities take (including set-up and clean-up); consider drive times, meals, and so on; and

16: PLANNING LINK

leave a "cushion" for the unexpected. If you could reserve even four hours out of eight for your top-priority activities, you would take control of your day and boost your productivity.

- **Setting agendas.** Planning what to say at a meeting or during a particular conversation makes those appointments more productive. Having an agenda (or talking points) helps ensure you discuss certain topics, makes you appear more professional, and shows respect for the other person(s)'s time.

- **Standardizing practices.** You can plan how to best accomplish recurring projects by developing standard practices. By creating, clarifying, and streamlining your processes and systems, you ensure greater accuracy, consistency, and efficiency—whether your company employs one person or one hundred thousand.

   You standardize practices in part by documenting them in some form, such as policy and procedures manuals, checklists, form letters, document templates, re-usable emails, and so on. They help you stop "re-inventing the wheel" and start driving.

- **Strategizing.** Strategic planning usually details how goals will be achieved over a period of years. It breaks large initiatives into sub-projects. Many organizations engage in formal strategic planning, but you can strategically plan your own job, career, and life, as well.

Effects of Planning on Productivity

Your Planning link has a great impact on your productivity. When it is strong enough, it enables you to:

- **Complete your important projects on time.** In the crush of requests, calls, emails, and other tasks, you may—without realizing it—continuously "back burner" your important projects. Project planning prevents this inadvertent procrastination by making your project-related tasks as bite-sized as your other calls and emails. (See box on previous page for details.) It also enables you to delegate pieces of the project to others, which may speed completion.

THE PRODUCTIVITY CHAIN

- **Reserve time for activities.** Scheduling activities on your calendar enables you to protect your time and tasks. It draws a theoretical line so less important activities cannot trespass. (A "strong enough" Boundary-setting link help you enforce it.)

    When Taylor, a professional speaker and consultant, booked a new workshop, she immediately blocked time on her calendar to prepare for the event. "If I didn't," she says, "I might accidentally fill my days with client appointments. I would have to work evenings or weekends to prepare the training. Been there, done that, won't do it again."

- **Counteract "magical" thinking.** Many people's perception of time relies on wishful thinking more than reality. They underestimate how long tasks take and overestimate the time they have, as Sean, an event coordinator, used to do.

    "I had unrealistic expectations of what I could do in one day," he admits. "My to-do list had twenty-five things I 'needed' to get done, and maybe an hour of free time during the day when I was not on the phone or in a meeting to do them."

    Through repeated practice, planning improves your estimates about how long activities take, how much time you have, what time "cushions" you need, and so on. This reality-based perspective counteracts magical thinking.

- **Turn goals into reality.** Planning helps you reserve the right amount of time for activities by taking you step-by-step through them. Let's say you want to get fit by exercising for an hour each day. Add getting dressed, driving to the gym, warming up, cooling down, stretching, showering, drying your hair, and dressing for work. That hour balloons into two (or more). Armed with that information, you can now allocate enough time to turn your exercise goal into reality (and keep your Health link strong).

- **Prioritize effectively.** Scheduling forces you to prioritize because it brings together your limited time with your unlimited tasks. It inspires you to ask important questions, such as: Is that project really going to help the bottom line? Could I meet them by phone or online instead of flying cross country? And so on.

16: PLANNING LINK

Item by item, you can begin to clear the clutter from your to-do list and calendar. (You strengthen your Decision-making and Goal-setting/Prioritization links with such questions, too.)

Dustin's Planning Story

Dustin, a publisher, used a schedule that enabled him to balance his two main responsibilities: meeting with—and signing—prospective authors, and overseeing operations. He set aside six standing appointment slots on his calendar for Monday through Thursday. Each day corresponded with a different part of the city. His target: to find prospects to fill those slots each week.

Dustin stuck with the plan. If someone in area "A" could not meet one week, he scheduled them for the next week, rather than moving them to a day when he was in a different neighborhood. Since his sales cycle was long and relationship-based, postponing meetings didn't harm his business.

Blocking out time in this way gave Dustin a much-needed sense of control over his calendar. It minimized his travel time and enabled his assistant to book appointments for him, too, since she could access his calendar.

Dustin's prospecting appointments acted like boulders in a stream. The rest of his appointments and activities flowed around them, but didn't dislodge them. Of course, Dustin could make an exception if he found someone worth it. "I like to use my Fridays for long weekends or strategic thinking," he notes, "but I can meet with someone that day if I choose." He rarely chooses it, though.

How to Strengthen Your Planning Link

When your Planning link is strong enough, it helps you use your time most wisely. If your Productivity Chain Analysis indicates you need to strengthen your Planning link, you might begin with these suggestions:

Break down the project breakdown.

Every productivity expert says you should break down a project into its parts so it doesn't seem so overwhelming. Then you can complete it bit by bit. This advice is absolutely sound. But what does that "breakdown" sound like? Another project in itself!

If the thought of project breakdown gives you a nervous breakdown, don't worry. Forget about all the steps you will take to complete the project. Just figure out the first one and put it on your task list. It's usually something simple, such as "Ask Martha, who did this last year, if she has any materials or suggestions."

One step will lead to another and before you know it, you are knee-deep in your project. At some point, you might do a little more project breakdown. By then, you will be so engaged in the project that the planning seems effortless.

Many people take this "just one step" approach to projects already. The tip, then, is to make it more intentional. "Own" it as a valid strategy, rather than feeling guilty for not beginning with a formal project breakdown.

Make appointments with your work.

You schedule appointments to meet with other people. Why not make an appointment to meet with yourself to work on a top-priority task? To make your "meeting" successful:

- **Be specific.** If you want to make prospecting calls starting at 10:00 AM, list the people you will contact, rather than just labeling the appointment "Calls." "Calls" is easy to dismiss. "Call Barbara Jones, Ira Mendez, and Shirley Grace" is not—especially if their numbers and your call agendas are right there, too.

- **Commit.** Give this appointment the same respect you would give a meeting with a client or supervisor. Show up on time and well-prepared.

- **Give your full attention.** Shut the door, turn off the email, put the phone on "do not disturb," and focus. If you met with a client, you would eliminate distractions. Your work on your client's behalf deserves that same attention. If you feel uneasy about this strategy, start with half-hour appointments. (And see Chapter 8: *Boundary-setting*.)

- **Stay flexible.** If you really cannot keep the appointment, treat it as you would any other: reschedule for the earliest available spot. Don't just cancel.

16: PLANNING LINK

- **Meet regularly.** Make these appointments with yourself a regular part of your day or week, maybe even a standing "date." They will likely be your most productive hours.

> *What may be done at any time will be done at no time.*
> Scottish Proverb

Plan early.

The sooner you start planning a project, the better. When you do, you feel calmer and can delegate more fully. You have more (and less expensive) options for event locations, caterers, flights, and contractors, for instance. You avoid rush fees, and so on.

Best of all, you have time to recover in case something goes wrong. The sooner you get your hands dirty in the project, the less mess you'll have later on.

Planning takes less time than you think, as Douglas, the financial advisor featured in Section I's case study, found. He wanted to hold a client-appreciation event, but planning seemed like a hassle. He had procrastinated for months.

I gave him a sheet of paper, a pen, and five minutes. It took Douglas four-and-a-half to identify the key activities needed and how he would delegate a few. Even though the plan was not "perfect," or even complete, it enabled him to take action after prolonged paralysis.

Keep your calendar simple.

To serve you well, your calendar must be clear, accurate, and easy to understand. If you have to try to remember whether that thirty-minute appointment labeled "Call Kay" is an actual scheduled appointment or just a reminder that you need to give her a ring sometime that day or week, your calendar does not work.

Andrew, a small business owner, used to put too many details on his calendar. "I found that if the calendar becomes cluttered, it detracts from its usefulness," he explains. "If it's too cluttered, I ignore it. It has to be simple and concise for me to pay attention and even understand it."

To simplify your calendar:

- Separate time-specific appointments from tasks that could be done at any time that day by using colors or labels or by keeping

the tasks in the "no time" part of that day's calendar.
- Distinguish between appointments with yourself and meetings with other people by using colors or labels. Self-appointments are slightly easier to reschedule.
- Enter accurate stop and start times. A two-hour meeting should take up two hours of space on the screen or page. A five-minute phone call that looks like it takes half an hour may cause you to think you have less time for other activities than you do.
- Use just one calendar, if possible. Multiple calendars (such as computer, wall, and planner) can leave you feeling fragmented and in constant danger of missing appointments. If nothing else, you waste time updating and checking them all.

16: PLANNING LINK

How Your Planning Link Interacts with Other Links

Here are examples of how this link interacts with the other eleven:

Boundary-setting: Scheduling appointments or milestones creates boundary lines on your calendar. Boundary-setting enables you to enforce those plans by not letting other activities trespass onto them.

Communication/Relationships: Planning often involves other people, requiring clear communication and cooperative relationships.

Decision-making: Planning begins with decisions: when to schedule what and for how long, what to include in a project plan, and so on.

Delegation: Planning early enough enables you to delegate more effectively.

Drive: Having a plan enables you to set aside time to maintain the order in your physical environment and computer. That order allows you to access your planning materials and information.

Goal-setting/Prioritization: Planning carves out the time to do the work to achieve goals. The limited hours in a day induce you to prioritize.

Health: Planning enables you to earmark time to take care of your health, e.g., to exercise, so other activities don't interfere.

Organization of Objects/Data: Being organized facilitates planning projects and events because it makes materials and information accessible.

Reinvention: Effective planning takes unexpected changes into account by creating contingency plans and padding time estimates.

Resources: Planning allows you to set aside time for professional or personal development activities.

Task/Project Management: Planning transforms the intentions of lists into the commitment of the calendar.

Link 17 Reinvention

"Any effective leader, any effective manager, really has to understand the dynamic nature of the world and not get comfortable with what is. Every day brings changes. Every aspect of how our business runs can change."
—Logan, CEO, waste disposal company

The Reinvention link concerns your response to, or creation of, change. Reinvention, on its own, refers to change you generate internally. As a link in the Productivity Chain, Reinvention also includes flexibility, which is how you handle external change that affects you. That change may occur in your department, organization, industry, society, the law, even your plan for the day.

Some changes are positive. Some are not. It can be difficult to determine at the outset which category applies to a particular situation. Regardless of your perception of the change, however, you can respond to it in ways that help you grow.

It helps to have a model for the change process in mind as you navigate through the experience of change. One simple, useful model is the 3A's: awareness, acceptance, and action. (See Chapter 20: *Overcome Your Productivity Myths* for details.)

This Link Adapts You

Your Reinvention link adapts you to change—whether the change is internal or external. When you respond flexibly and successfully to change, your personal power flows. It is human nature, after all, to grow. Resisting change in destructive ways, such as denial or stagnation, stifles your productivity power.

17: REINVENTION LINK

Examples of Reinvention
Reinvention refers to changes that you initiate or make yourself. The word itself implies the need for creativity, ingenuity, and **invention**. Reinvention takes many forms, including:
- Adjusting or replacing practices that no longer work;
- Abandoning something that **does** work in favor of something that will work better;
- Adopting a new business model;
- Rebranding your business;
- Changing your career;
- Becoming the person who...[*exercises, stands up for herself, leads others*—you fill in the blank].

Examples of Flexibility
External change occurs with the speed of text messages these days. Flexibility is your ability to manage the change in positive, resourceful ways. It enables you to stay current and relevant. Flexibility takes many forms, such as:
- Adopting a cautiously positive attitude when another company purchases yours;
- Greeting unexpected visitors graciously and adjusting your plans;
- Seeing your assistant's quitting as an opportunity to hire someone with a better skill set;
- Asking a colleague to run your meeting when a client makes an urgent and unanticipated demand that only you can handle.

Effects of Reinvention on Productivity
When your Reinvention link is strong enough, you focus your energy on your work, instead of on your responses to the changes it entails. You can:
- **Improve systems.** Every process can be simplified, tweaked, or modified. A series of small, incremental changes over time

creates deep and enduring transformation, as Kaizen[14] (the process improvement strategy made famous by Japanese car manufacturers) and recent brain research[15] show. It simply requires willingness to keep getting a little better all the time.

- **Respond, rather than react, to surprises.** Carleen, a graphic designer who works out of her home, illustrates the benefits of responding flexibly to the unexpected. "Today I had the best of intentions," she says. "I got back from my lunch, and found the dog had been bit by something in her eye. Instead of finishing the day as I had planned, I took the dog to the vet.

    "Before, it would have been a disaster," Carleen admits. "I'd think, 'I don't have time for this!' Now, I just deal with it and move on. Everything will eventually get done. No more staying up until twelve or one o'clock in the morning, either. I have a different perspective now." That new perspective enables her to handle changes in plans without wasting energy or losing motivation. She makes sure that everything that must be done, gets done, and lets go of the rest.

- **Remain viable.** Today's workplace demands flexibility and resilience. Your willingness to approach new tools, situations, and goals with a positive attitude reflects the humility necessary for growth. It also keeps you employed. If you are mentally too old to learn new tricks, you will not last—regardless of your actual age.

Alan's Reinvention Story

Alan was a sales consultant who had served customers in his large territory for fifteen years. Always a top producer, he had become troubled in recent years by his inability to give some of his clients the attention he once had. "I felt guilty," he says. "Especially when they complained that they didn't see me as often as before. I hate feeling that I'm not giving my best."

Alan prided himself on his customer service, although in the beginning the service was simple. "When I started," he explains, "I was kind of like a milkman. I'd drive my route, hitting the same customers every couple weeks, filling their small orders."

17: REINVENTION LINK

As he acquired more accounts, he called on some formerly top-tier customers less frequently. They had slipped to the middle or lower tiers in terms of orders. "I started off with a three-week call cycle," he notes. "Then it was four weeks, then five. Now it's a six-week cycle that includes new areas. I may change it again after reviewing my progress."

Over the years, Alan's customers, their needs, and his products changed. So did Alan's role. "Now I'm a consultant," he says. "I spend more time on fewer accounts. Their orders are huge and I do everything I can to solve their problems and add any value I can."

> While his role had changed, Alan's expectations of himself had not.

While his role and title had changed, Alan's expectations of himself had not. Part of him still thought he should give the milkman treatment to all his customers and see them as often as he used to—especially the ones who had been with him from the start.

His inner conflict troubled him for months until he finally accepted his current business model without reservation. That meant not beating himself up for not giving all his customers equal time since it wasn't sensible or even feasible. In the end, Alan didn't need to change his call schedule—just his mindset.

How to Strengthen Your Reinvention Link

If your Productivity Chain Analysis indicates you need to strengthen your Reinvention link, begin right away. Strengthening **any** link requires change. If you can become more comfortable with change, you can more easily strengthen other links in your Chain, too. To improve your Reinvention link:

Become a continuous improvement machine.

Sustainably high productivity requires you to practice continuous improvement. What works today may not work tomorrow. Your skills grow, your clients change, your opportunities increase, and technology advances. Consistently successful professionals readily shed what no longer fits and adopt what does.

"I'm always thinking 'How can this be improved upon?'" explains Karen, the CEO featured in the case study at the end of

Section III. "I just enjoy it. It's not about me not being satisfied. It's about growing and progressing. I just can't stand being stagnant. It's unhealthy. Everything is evolving and growing and changing, whether it's your personal life or business. It doesn't work to just stand still."

Be ready to change your self-image.

Sometimes reinvention requires your self-image to change, if your current view no longer fits who you are or who you need to be.

Reeza's Story

Reeza was the manager at an accounting firm. For two years, she had supported, cajoled, and coddled her direct-report Les, hoping she could "grow" him into being a more careful and motivated supervisor. She saw herself as a loyal, fair manager who nurtured people. "I knew I needed to fire him," she says, "but I didn't want to give up on him."

Finally, she reached a breaking point. Les' carelessness made her look bad. Even worse, it hurt the entire organization, costing—or threatening to cost—tens of thousands of dollars. It also set a bad example for his staff. Reeza realized she had to change since Les wouldn't.

She chose to see "holding people accountable" as a way to nurture them and their coworkers. This new view of the word, and therefore of herself, gave her the permission she needed to fire Les. And she did.

Expect the unexpected.

You can expect that life will toss you "unexpected" curveballs. You can handle them more flexibly by adding a "cushion" of time in your work day for them. Expecting the unexpected also helps you remind yourself of potential delays, such as long lines at the store, the server possibly going down, or so-and-so being absent.

Bringing those negative possibilities to mind does not make you a pessimist. Instead, it helps you respond to such glitches with a sunnier outlook. It also inspires you to avoid "last-minute-itis" and encourages you to think about how you might handle any contingency.

17: REINVENTION LINK

Embrace external change.

When your firm announces a new initiative, or when a law affecting your industry passes, look for the opportunities created. Change is difficult, but you can adapt more easily when you focus on potential benefits, as Neta did.

Neta's Story

Neta was a psychotherapist with her own office and staff. Over time, she realized that insurance companies reimbursed her services for less and less. She knew the trend would continue, and she seized the opportunity to change her focus.

Unlike many of her therapist colleagues, she did not bury her head in the sand, complain as earnings declined, or leave the industry. Instead, she went back to school, got an advanced credential in her field, and began doing forensic work.

In addition to the family counseling she had practiced for years, Neta testified in legal cases about child custody. Eventually, she moved into jury selection, as well. Her earnings skyrocketed. By embracing her changed marketplace in ways that aligned with her interests and values, Neta's career thrived.

THE PRODUCTIVITY CHAIN

How Your Reinvention Link Interacts with Other Links

Here are examples of how this link interacts with the other eleven:

Boundary-setting: Modifying your boundaries depending on the circumstances, the people involved, the level of familiarity, and so on, can be an important skill. It reflects an ability to adapt to change.

Communication/Relationships: Embracing or resisting change may alter your relationships with others, depending on their approaches to the situation.

Decision-making: Reinventing yourself successfully begins with a decision to adapt to new conditions, whether they originate inside you or come from your environment.

Delegation: Resisting change or latching onto it deeply affects the people who report to you or try to help you.

Drive: Cultivating an attitude that embraces change enhances your ability to adapt to change.

Goal-setting/Prioritization: Changing circumstances inspire you to adapt your priorities accordingly.

Health: Changing mental and physical health creates an opportunity to practice being adaptable and flexible.

Organization of Objects/Data: Keeping your objects and data organized requires constant adaptation to changing circumstances. "Hot" files, for example, cool quickly, to be replaced by newer projects.

Planning: Effective planning takes unexpected changes into account by creating contingency plans and padding time estimates.

Resources: Overcoming a reflexive resistance to change and new tools enables you to stay relevant and current.

Task/Project Management: As change occurs, you have to be able to revise, and even to let go of, projects and tasks if necessary.

Link

 **Resources**

"I spend a lot of money and time in continuing education. I know many people who don't. They're doing a fifth of the business that I'm doing, and they 'don't have time' to learn. It probably is true: because of what they're doing, they don't have time."
—Taylor, professional speaker and consultant

The Resources link contains all the assets and raw materials—both internal and external—that help you accomplish your work. It differs from most other links in two respects. First, it includes factors that may fall outside your control, such as the speed of your company's server.

Second, it addresses the content of your job—***what*** you do. Most of the other links address ***how*** you do it. In that respect, the strength of your Resources link depends in part on your current position at your particular company. Other aspects of this link, however, are "portable" and fully within your power to change.

This Link Equips You

Your Resources link equips you with all the tools you need to perform productively. These tools include self-knowledge, job skills, support personnel, equipment, materials, actual tools, technology, and so on.

The right tools enhance your personal power by focusing it where it has the most influence—on your efforts to achieve your goals. Your power becomes stifled by frustration when you have to struggle to obtain needed resources or do without.

THE PRODUCTIVITY CHAIN

> **An Ax or a Chainsaw**
>
> To appreciate the impact of the Resources link on your productivity, picture this scene:[16] A man, dripping sweat, chops down a tree with an ax, a forest of trees behind him.
>
> His buddy, standing nearby with a chainsaw, says, "You could clear this forest faster with this." "Maybe," the ax-wielder replies, "but I don't have time to learn how. I'm too busy chopping down these trees."
>
> The irony is clear. With this new tool, he could accomplish his project much more quickly, even with the training time. Now substitute "assistant," "methods," or "software" for "ax." What could **you** do with better tools?

Types of Resources that Affect Productivity

Some of your work tools reside within you; others come from your organization. The resources at your disposal are too numerous to list, but the following categories are key to productivity:

- **Self-Knowledge:** This knowledge includes understanding your personality traits, processing modalities, various strengths and weaknesses, personal preferences, talents, and so on. Self-knowledge helps you select a job that fits. (See Appendix C: *Productivity-Related Terms* to learn more about some of these factors.)

- **Job-Related Knowledge:** This knowledge includes job-specific information (e.g., maritime law for that kind of attorney), how to cut "red tape," developments in your industry, and so on.

- **Job-Related Skills:** These skills include negotiation, sales, diagnostics, management, software, and so on—whatever your role requires.

- **Organizational Support:** Support from your organization includes availability and/or quality of technology, support personnel, furnishings, equipment, building, and so on. Receiving temporary assistance from an intern is helpful, for instance, but getting ongoing support from a trained, dedicated assistant is even better.

18: RESOURCES LINK

Effects of Resources on Productivity

The Resources link affects productivity in many ways. When it is strong enough, your Resources link enables you to:

- **Accomplish your own work more quickly.** Knowing and relying on the right people, having the equipment you need (in good working order), and keeping your skills up-to-date all help you produce results with less time and energy.

    Laura, a sales representative, could delegate more effectively once she found the right human resources in her company's "back office." "Before, I'd call and sit on hold," she says. "Then I found the good people and got their email addresses. Now I contact them directly."

- **Learn faster.** Self-knowledge speeds learning—a critical skill in our "knowledge work" economy. You can understand and assimilate new information, systems, and routines faster when you know and apply your strengths and preferences. If you learn best by doing, for example, you might work with a trainer one-on-one, rather than read a book on the subject.

- **Take an entire organization's productivity to a higher level.** New facilities or technology can enhance the outlook and output of everyone in an organization. Profession-specific or custom-designed software, for instance, can be expensive but sometimes worth it.

Accounting Software Story

One accounting firm client purchased software to process tax returns and audits digitally and provided its accountants with three flat-screen monitors each. The accountants could then view last year's return, this year's return, and their email and calendar simultaneously.

With these new resources, processing times and paper costs plummeted. So did stress levels. No more walking to the distant file room (or waiting for delivery). No more misplaced files or costly searches. In addition, the new software enabled managers to better allocate work and ensure accountants did assignments first-in, first-out—regardless of how messy or difficult a particular return or audit. Their customer service therefore improved, as well.

Perhaps the greatest evidence of the effectiveness of this new software was the quiet hum of activity during tax season. There were fewer crises, fewer meltdowns, and calmer employees. Best of all, there were more error-free returns filed on time.

Anne's Resources Story

Lack of organizational resources limits the productivity of many workers. People share assistants or go without. They make do with outdated software programs and slow servers. The list could go on.

Sometimes, however, the lack of support is self-imposed. Anne, a vice president at a telecom company, noticed the CEO's assistant, Martha, helping another member of the executive team. Anne felt jealous because she needed help, too. Unlike her fellow VP, however, Anne had never asked for it.

Shortly thereafter, Anne approached Martha herself. Martha happily completed a long-delayed project for Anne and took over a duty that Anne should have delegated long ago. Once Anne stopped trying to do everything herself, she began to realize what greater support could mean to her productivity.

Within months, she hired an additional staff person to work for her full time. She even began succession planning, which would involve hiring a second-in-command. These resources helped Anne, but they helped her company even more because of what they allowed Anne to accomplish.

How to Strengthen Your Resources Link

There are almost as many ways to strengthen your Resources link as there are resources. If your Productivity Chain Analysis indicates you need to strengthen your Resources link, you might begin with these suggestions:

Commit to professional development.

Develop a plan to develop yourself professionally. You might skim a monthly trade journal, follow an industry leader through social media, attend a week of training every year, or pursue a credential. Whatever you decide, commit to it. Staying current and relevant increases your value to your organization and your clients.

18: RESOURCES LINK

Dustin, the publisher from Chapter 16, leverages his Resources link regularly and it has paid off. "Ten percent of my time has got to be spent in some kind of training, practicing, or self-development," he says. "I'm probably ten years ahead of where I would have been if I didn't have all the training I have."

Keep learning how to really get things done.

In every line of work, there are three ways to do things: the "official," correct way; the absolutely wrong way; and the smartest and best way. That third method accomplishes your goal, cuts through red tape, involves the best people, and occasionally stretches—but never breaks—the rules. It's the productivity equivalent of taking the quickest route on a map. Learn and apply that method for your own line of work.

Maximize the software you use regularly.

If you use a software program on a daily or weekly basis and you are not highly proficient already, learn how to use it more fully. Most people harness just a fraction of their technology's power.

One easy way to begin: right-click anything in a Windows-based software program and then select one of the options that appears. Try it out. See what's there. Then right-click something else tomorrow. Or read a short section of the Help index. In a few months, you will be the resident guru for that software.

Alternatively, hire a trainer. "I knew we weren't fully using the software we had in front of us," notes Robert, an executive for a military contractor. "I knew it was capable of more. I just didn't realize how much more until someone showed me."

Leverage your preferences and personality to accomplish more.

The more you know about yourself, the more you can apply that knowledge to learn, work, and relate to others more effectively. Take the personality traits of introversion and extraversion, for example. Extraverts draw energy from being around other people. Introverts recharge their batteries by being alone.

Use your preference to plan your day. As an extravert, you might walk around the office or schedule lunch with a friend if you

THE PRODUCTIVITY CHAIN

have been tied to your desk alone for too long. As an introvert, on the other hand, you might schedule time alone after a staff meeting so you can decompress and energetically regroup.

How Your Resources Link Interacts with Other Links

Here are examples of how this link interacts with the other eleven:

Boundary-setting: Setting boundaries enables you to protect your area's critical tools, equipment, personnel, etc., when competition for organizational resources exists.

Communication/Relationships: Communicating assertively enables you to request and obtain necessary training and resources. Leveraging relationships may help, as well.

Decision-making: Obtaining additional knowledge, skills, and other resources requires a decision to act.

Delegation: Having someone to assist you is a valuable resource. You may also delegate to someone the responsibility of obtaining necessary resources, e.g., purchasing new equipment.

Drive: Having sufficient resources contributes to a positive attitude. Self-awareness and self-knowledge enables you to better manage your motivation.

Goal-setting/Prioritization: Continuing your professional education or obtaining a certain tool begins with setting that goal and then making it a priority.

Health: Maintaining your health requires you to tap into resources, such as physicians, nutritional information, and classes (e.g., yoga or kickboxing). It also draws on your own self-knowledge regarding preferences, and so on.

Organization of Objects/Data: Being organized, especially when it involves liberal use of the trash can, saves on storage costs and replacement costs of resources. It facilitates professional development by making reference files accessible.

Planning: Planning allows you to set aside time for professional or personal development activities.

Reinvention: Overcoming a reflexive resistance to change and new tools enables you to stay relevant and current.

Task/Project Management: Obtaining an advanced credential or learning new sales techniques are actually projects, involving multiple tasks, which you can manage alongside your other projects and tasks.

Link 19

Task/Project Management

"My list is detailed, but not too detailed. It reminds me of things I have to do during the day. It used to be, when I'd sit at home or I'd lie in bed, I'd think, 'I forgot to do this' or 'I didn't call that person.' I'd get aggravated with myself. Now I put it on the list and I run the list every morning. It makes life easier."
—Ashley, chief operations officer

The Task/Project Management link identifies, clarifies, and reminds you of all you need to do. It enables you to prioritize and track your work efficiently and effectively. If you are accustomed to jumping in and working without stepping back to consider your overall workload and status of projects, taking a little time each day and week to manage your tasks and projects will prove invaluable to your productivity.

This Link Advances Your Work

Your Task/Project Management link advances your work—and your career—task by task, project by project. Through monitoring, managing, and adjusting your workload, you gain power over it. In fact, this link deepens your personal power because it enables you to control your activities, rather than feel controlled by them.

Tasks and Projects: Your To-Do's

In the Productivity Chain, "task" and "project" have very specific meanings. They can be work-related or personal. Combined, your tasks and projects comprise your "to-do's."

- **Task:** A task is any one-step action or activity, such as writing an email, making a phone call, or doing a simple (though possibly time-consuming) report.

A task is usually one small piece of a project, role, responsibility, or function, but it might seem to stand alone, such as when a friend contacts you for a job. Returning that call is a task that actually relates to your role as friend. (Helping that friend get a job is a project if you take more action.)

- **Project:** A project is "any desired result that requires more than one action step"[17] to achieve. This definition (from David Allen's *Getting Things Done*) means that serving each client, converting each prospect, and managing each company-wide initiative is a project. Your projects include those you delegate to others and those you execute yourself.

Projects vary greatly in size. Ordering products online exemplifies a mini-project. The tasks it requires: order, wait for order to arrive, put products away, and address any errors. Larger projects—such as planning a fundraising event, preparing for a certification exam, or completing a complex report—contain more tasks and even sub-projects.

In a sense, your roles and job duties may be considered ongoing projects. Solving a problem for a client, for instance, is a project if it requires multiple phone calls, emails, and conversations, etc. Counseling an employee and then following up with her over the next six months is a project, as well.

Traditional, large-scale Project Management, such as that used in manufacturing, software development, and construction, has a very specialized meaning. It actually occurs through coordination of all twelve links. In fact, that kind of "Project Management" is its own profession and so falls outside the scope of this discussion. Even professional project managers, however, need an effective ***personal*** task and project management system.

Effects of Task/Project Management on Productivity

Task/Project Management profoundly affects your productivity. When that link is strong enough, it enables you to:

19: TASK/PROJECT MANAGEMENT LINK

- **Do your important work.** An effective task management system contains only next-step actions. That means your work is broken into bite-sized pieces you can actually accomplish without any further preparation or decision-making. This action-orientation enables you to complete bigger projects one step at a time without procrastination. (See Chapter 16: *Planning* for details about breaking projects into tasks.)

- **Keep things from "slipping through the cracks."** A strong, functional task/project management system reminds you of what you need to do in a way that encourages you to act. It "alarms" you at the right times and keeps you from getting overwhelmed by a heavy workload.

- **Clear your mental clutter.** When you use a system you trust, your brain stops running its distracting "Remember to do this"/"You forgot to do that!" program. Without that mental clutter, you can concentrate on your actual work. (And fall asleep more easily.)

- **Reduce your physical clutter.** Your task/project management system—not your files or papers—reminds you of what you need to do. You can then find "homes" for the files and papers without worrying that you will forget an important task. (This kind of system does not work for everyone, however.)

- **Prioritize and plan effectively.** You can make sound decisions about how to spend your time only when you can consider all your options. That's what your task/project management system helps you do.

Dez's Task/Project Management Story

Dez, a loan officer, felt distracted by his to-do's. When meeting with clients, part of his mind kept returning to the stacks on his desk and the hastily scrawled notes tucked beside his keyboard. "They reminded me of all the stuff I haven't gotten to," he says. "They made me nervous because I didn't know what was in them."

Designing and using a system he trusted eased his mind and enabled him to serve his clients better. Now he advises everyone to "Get it out of your head. Put it in a system. I don't want to keep task reminders in my mind anymore." His mental clarity has become as necessary to him as bathing.

Dez can tell the difference when he doesn't use his system diligently. "I get kind of anxious," he admits. "When I haven't placed things on my task list where they're supposed to be, and too much is coming at me, and I'm trying to remember it all, it gets a little chaotic." It reminds him of how he used to feel all the time.

Although it took a while to adjust to reviewing his task list each day and deciding what to tackle first, he has come to love it. "I actually look forward every morning to checking my list," he admits. It reassures him that he won't forget something important.

His strong Reinvention link has led Dez to improve and adapt his system continuously. "While I'm putting tasks onto my list, I'm thinking, 'How do I make that better?'" he says. "Or 'What's the quickest way to look at them?' Or 'What's the best way to put information in?'"

He has even trained his staff to help him. "The people I worked with daily sent tasks to me all the time. I started teaching them a format for the email subject line so I had fewer adjustments to make on my end when I dragged the email onto my Task list," he explains. "I asked them to put the name and phone number of the person I should call, for example." Since Dez got hundreds of emails daily, shaving a few seconds off each one had a large cumulative effect.

How to Strengthen Your Task/Project Management Link

There is no one-size-fits-all way for handling your projects and tasks. Even those who advocate a specific system usually end up using it idiosyncratically themselves. You need customization because the way you work is unique. It applies only to you at this specific time, holding this particular position. It will change.

> There is no one-size-fits-all way for handling your projects and tasks.

Still, certain strategies or principles can make any task and project management practice more useful. If your Productivity Chain Analysis indicates you need to strengthen your Task/Project Management link, you might begin with these suggestions:

19: TASK/PROJECT MANAGEMENT LINK

Centralize your system.

You need a central location to stockpile your ideas and obligations. It's the only way you can prioritize successfully and make rational decisions about your time. Having an inventory of all your to-do's in one place also encourages you to delegate and to let go of relatively less important tasks and projects. (They can only seem less important when compared to the rest.)

To make it work, find ways to add to your central system no matter where you are. If a great idea occurs to you while driving, for example, call your work number and leave yourself a message. If you think of a solution to a problem as you get ready for bed, send yourself an email or jot down a note and leave it by your car keys or the door.

Use lists—whatever type you prefer.

A central system requires lists of some kind. Lists can be paper-based, using a planner, spiral notebook, index cards, labeled folders, or sticky notes. They can be electronic, managed with a specialized software program or phone app. They can be tasks marked on your digital calendar.

Even a designated stack of files on your desk can be a "list" if you know what's in it and review the files regularly. High-tech or low-tech makes no difference. All that matters is that your list suits *you*. Its value depends on your using it faithfully.

"There are things that make your brain go, 'Oh, I like that,'" says Alice, an ad executive. "For me, writing with a pen is one of those things, but writing on the computer is one, too. I've blended both in my system, and it works for me."

Jan, a trial attorney, uses her "hot" client folders as a bulky kind of list. "I look at every case file in my office before I go home on Friday," she explains. "I open it up and say, 'Okay, that's right. I'm meeting with this person next week.' It reassures me that I have control." That's what effective lists do.

Separate projects, tasks, and ideas.

To be most functional, your system needs at least three lists: projects, tasks, and ideas. Projects are your larger goals and objectives; tasks are one-step actions. Both represent your obligations—or at least your intentions. Ideas, on the other hand, are merely possibilities.

If you keep all three on the same list, you will almost always do the easy tasks, ignore the complicated projects, and feel guilty for not implementing the ideas. That system doesn't work.

Separate lists make it easier to function. You operate off your task list each day. Your project list helps ensure your daily tasks reflect those projects and move you towards goal achievement. Your idea list, finally, allows you to choose which to act on and which to abandon without guilt.

"It's fuzzy thinking to mix a project with a task," asserts Logan, CEO of a waste disposal company. "Projects don't go onto a task list. They need to be broken down and their tasks go on the list. Until then, it's hard to make progress."

Review your lists often.

Effective systems require regular reviews. Reviews ensure your lists are accurate and up-to-date. They also enable you to determine which tasks, projects, and ideas you should focus on, discard, scale back, activate, delegate, or put on the back burner. In this way, you manage your workload—the purpose of this link.

> Regular reviews keep your lists from becoming overgrown, inaccurate, and unmanageable.

Without regular reviews, your lists become overgrown, inaccurate, and unmanageable. You stop using them. Reviewing them often, however, allows you to funnel everything through them—a one-stop shop for all your to-do's.

A simple, centralized, often-reviewed system reassures your brain that you won't forget anything—reducing your mental clutter and giving you peace of mind.

19: TASK/PROJECT MANAGEMENT LINK

How Your Task/Project Management Link Interacts with Other Links

Here are examples of how this link interacts with the other eleven:

Boundary-setting: Distinguishing between tasks and projects essentially draws a boundary line between the two; that clarity improves the effectiveness of any task and project management system.

Communication/Relationships: Many projects involve other people and success depends upon clear communication and positive relationships.

Decision-making: Managing tasks and projects effectively requires constant decisions about what action to take with each document, email, and so on.

Delegation: Having clarity about all your tasks and projects enables (and motivates) you to delegate.

Drive: Viewing your task and project management system in a positive light contributes to its effectiveness because you are more likely to use it regularly, which is what makes it work.

Goal-setting/Prioritization: Collecting your tasks and projects in one system enables you to prioritize them effectively—which includes matching your priorities with your larger goals.

Health: Losing weight, training for a race, or staying fit are all projects for you to manage. An effective task and project management system, meanwhile, helps you work more effectively and sleep more soundly.

Organization of Objects/Data: Organizing objects and data often occurs in conjunction with creating task and project lists. A paper can be tossed or filed once the relevant action goes on a list.

Planning: Planning transforms the intentions of lists into the commitment of the calendar.

Reinvention: As change occurs, you have to be able to revise, and even to let go of, projects and tasks if necessary.

Resources: Obtaining an advanced credential or learning new sales techniques are actually projects, involving multiple tasks, which you can manage alongside your other projects and tasks.

THE PRODUCTIVITY CHAIN

Your Next Step:
Examine Your Own Productivity Myths

The Productivity Chain concept can transform the way you evaluate and improve your work performance. For many people, however, long-standing beliefs about productivity and time may keep them from embracing this model.

Habits of thought can be difficult to overcome, especially when popular culture reinforces them every day. You can begin by learning about the myths and the realities they disguise. The next section, *Productivity Myths*, explores both.

CASE STUDY: BUTCH

Butch's Story

Butch's experience shows the power of strengthening a single link, Delegation. It took his performance to a much higher level, improving his staff's productivity—and his relationship with them—in the process.

SUMMARY

The Professional: Butch is a litigation attorney

Strong Links: Drive, Resources

Solutions that Worked—Strengthening the Weak Link:

- Delegation: Let go, even of tasks he thinks he can do better.

Butch is a high-powered, highly-sought-after trial attorney. His success, however, came at a hefty price. He worked very long hours, which took a toll on his family and himself. He hired me when he realized that he couldn't achieve a more fulfilling personal life if he continued on his current path.

His Productivity Chain assessment revealed a broken Delegation link. He had associate attorneys, a paralegal, and a top-notch assistant working for him. But Butch believed that "if you want something done right, you have to do it yourself." As a result, he did as much himself as he could. It was exhausting.

> *I see it, I assign it, and I get it out.*
> — Butch, attorney

"I think my entire career until the past few years, I was stymied by the fact that I never really trusted people to delegate to them," he reflects. "When I was younger and angrier, I would see some work that didn't meet my perfectionistic standard, and I would redo the whole thing. I'd think, 'It would have been quicker and faster if I had just done it to begin with.' Today, there's no more of that. I see it, I assign it and I get it out."

His reluctance to delegate much injured his relationships with his staff. "I hired the team. I thought they were going to do everything I needed," he explains, "but they didn't, because I wouldn't delegate the responsibility to them. As a result, I was constantly upset with them."

THE PRODUCTIVITY CHAIN

The light began to dawn that he, not they, had the problem after he saw how much they accomplished while he was on vacation. "I realized my team was far more capable than I had allowed myself to believe. I had to let go of some of the things that I would have taken on before," he admits. He began sharing his work and quickly realized the benefits—more cases closed, more motivated and engaged employees, and less stress.

> *I no longer support this absurd notion of grandiosity where I do all the work.*
> Butch, attorney

Delegating has enabled Butch to spend his time most profitably, focusing on his strengths. "The toughest thing for me to do is start a document," he says. "So my paralegal does it. Put the draft in front of me, and I can refine it and it's done. If I had to get that initial document into existence myself, that'd be a wall I'd still be trying to breach."

Butch has a new relationship with his staff now. "I no longer support this absurd notion of grandiosity where I do all the work. Now I delegate, and we work with each other. They do not work *for* me, they work **with** me, and everybody is allowed to question anybody's idea about anything."

Placing greater value on his team's contributions has produced winning results. "I rely on my paralegals much more heavily than in the past," Butch notes. "They substantively participate in case analysis, plans, and theme, and become very invested in it. They want to win. It is a potent recipe for success." They experience a lot of it.

Better delegation has helped Butch's personal life, too. "Now, I rely on other people to do different facets of trial preparation. That allows me to be ready and not have to work until 3:00 or 4:30 the morning before the first day of trial. I'm home by 7:00 every night now." His wife and children appreciate that.

Learning to delegate and repairing his relationships did not happen overnight. It has been a process of acceptance for Butch. "I perpetually fight that idea that nobody can do it better than I can," he reveals. "When I delegate and don't get the results I want, there's always that burning feeling, 'I should have done it.'

"Then I let go. I tell myself, 'What's done is done and I'm going to go forward.' And I'm still winning cases." For a litigation attorney, that productivity is all that matters.

Section III
Productivity Myths

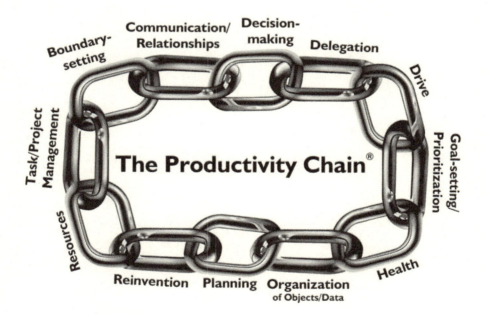

Productivity Myths Introduction

The Productivity Chain model offers a new, more effective approach to improving your productivity. It reframes your situation, defining your problems in ways that pinpoint solutions and clarifying that your problems—and solutions—exist within your power and control.

But the Productivity Chain only works if you let go of less empowering problem/solution perspectives, which may be easier said than done. The media and culture reinforce many mistaken ideas about the source of your productivity struggles—most of which leave your without power to improve them.

These habits of thought can be difficult to shake. Developed over many years, they may lurk below your conscious awareness, influencing your behavior even though your rational mind recognizes their inaccuracies.

If you act on them, these myths prevent you from applying the Productivity Chain model and developing more effective work habits. They stifle your productivity because you waste time pursuing them. Most damaging of all, they threaten your peace of mind if you blame yourself when they fail to help you accomplish your goals.

Your Behavior Reveals What You Believe

This section strips the myths bare. Seeing them in black and white, perhaps worded in a certain way, you may find them easy to dismiss. You "know better" than to believe any of them. Your actions, however, may say otherwise. As you read about the myths, let your **behavior**, not your brain, reveal what you believe—and to what extent you believe it.

THE PRODUCTIVITY CHAIN

> **Exercise: What's Your Mythology?**
>
> Before reading about the myths in detail, take a moment to scan the list below. Some myths might echo thoughts you have had over the years. These might be your personal productivity myths, so put a check by them.
>
> **Productivity Myths**
> ___I can do it all.
> ___I need more time.
> ___I need to work harder.
> ___I need to get more organized.
> ___I should be able to handle everything myself.
> ___I can make up for lost time.
> ___I can't play until my work is done.
> ___I am not naturally productive.
> ___Others can make up for what I lack.
> ___Others are the problem.
> ___My productivity problem has no upside.
> ___The problem will get better by itself.

Most beliefs aren't black and white. You probably don't operate out of a particular myth all the time, for instance. Still, even partial belief can inhibit your productivity if it affects your behavior.

Keep an Open Mind

As you read—or decide to read—about a myth, keep an open mind. Some myths' "names" might be comments you've made or heard others make. Others might seem odd or intriguing, even off-putting, at first. Begin reading, though, and you may recognize your own thoughts and behaviors on unexpected pages.

This collection of myths comes from years of listening to and observing clients and others. These are the myths that have impaired their productivity or kept them from improving it.

A few of the myths share a common theme, but each variation has its own nuances and solution. One version may resonate with you in ways that another does not.

Before you begin reading about the myths, do the "What's Your Mythology?" exercise for a quick self-assessment (box on previous page). You might do the same exercise ***after*** reading these chapters to see if your responses change.

Mythic Strategies and Summaries

Each myth's chapter contains valuable information designed with quick reading in mind, including:

- a description of the myth and the harm it does;
- a specific, productivity-enhancing strategy for letting it go;
- real-world examples;
- a summary box on the last page that specifies the myth, the reality, the harm caused by the myth, the Productivity Chain (PC) Solution, and the link(s) that need strengthening in order to resolve that myth.

In addition, the next chapter (Chapter 20: *Overcome Your Productivity Myths*) explains a simple model of the change process (the 3A's) that can guide your progress as you let go of your personal productivity myths and adopt the more empowering Productivity Chain perspective. You can actually begin that process just by reading about the myths.

20 Overcome Your Productivity Myths

You loosen the grip of your personal productivity myths by first realizing they *are* myths. That acknowledgement takes away some of their power to blind you. Next, you apply the 3A's.

The 3A's

The 3A's is a simple model of the change process that comes from Al-Anon, the twelve-step program for family and friends of alcoholics. Decades of experience among its members have proven its usefulness. The 3A's are:

1. **Awareness:** Awareness counteracts denial. When you catch yourself being influenced by a myth—when you are aware—you have greater leverage to change your thoughts and behavior.

2. **Acceptance:** Acceptance acknowledges what is—not what was or could be. It doesn't require you to like or agree with what is; just admit reality. It is the key that unlocks the door to lasting change. Accept that you believe your myths, though you think you shouldn't. If you resist or deny them, the myths persist.

3. **Action:** Effective action becomes possible only after awareness and acceptance exist. You don't have to be "over" the myth before you change your behavior, however—just aware and accepting of your current status.

   In fact, your actions can change your mind. Begin acting "as if" you do not believe the myth. Eventually, your changed behavior turns your "act" into reality. You "act yourself into right thinking," as they say.

The 3A "stages" occur on many levels. They flow in order at the highest level. You can see the progression when looking back, years

20: OVERCOME YOUR PRODUCTIVITY MYTHS

later at a significant change, for example. On any given day, however, you might move back and forth among all the stages, depending on the situation or your mood.

Emily's 3A's Story

Emily, who owns a retail carpeting business, discovered through her Productivity Chain Self-Assessment that her fragile Boundary-setting and Goal-setting/Prioritization links contributed to her sense that she was constantly in a rush and putting out fires.

She almost never said "no" to requests and often took on new responsibilities without being asked. Her to-do list overflowed. She had difficulty doing that work because she couldn't say "no" to interruptions, either—regardless of their relative importance.

Upon reflection, Emily realized that her belief in the myth that she could "do it all" (Chapter 21) kept her from flexing her boundary-setting muscles. Intellectually, she knew she was only human, but all those "yeses" said otherwise. She felt she had to let go of this myth or she would keep operating in crisis mode.

So she applied the 3A's. Emily became more ***Aware*** of how she let email and phone calls and other people's wishes—not her own priorities—drive her behavior. She realized it made her feel pulled in all directions and out of control. It became painful to watch herself do it because she also became more aware of the toll it took on her family, her peace of mind, and her physical health.

She practiced ***Acceptance*** by forgiving herself for taking on so much in the first place. She recognized how easy it was to fall into that people-pleasing trap—and that she could get out.

She started to let go of the "I can do it all" myth by ***Acting*** as if she had human limitations. That meant prioritizing and setting boundaries. She started to review and prioritize her task list before checking email—something she wouldn't need to do if she could do it all. She also bit her tongue whenever she wanted to "help" someone who didn't really need her help. Finally, she set a six-month moratorium on taking on any new personal commitments.

Sometimes Emily still tried to pack too much into a given day—trying to do it all. Productivity myths die hard. When that happened, she just returned to 3A's and focused on her weak links. Greater productivity, control, and calmness always ensued.

Myth 21 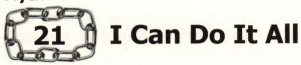 I Can Do It All

"It's ridiculous and arrogant of me to think I can 'do it all,' but really, that's what I try to do. I always cram in just one more thing. I run around late and stressed, trying to be superwoman and feeling guilty that I'm not."
—Barbara, chief financial officer

Like it or not, you cannot do everything you want to do, need to do, or think you "should" do. That's not a problem necessarily; just a reality. The real problem is believing—or acting as if you believe—you **can** do it all. This belief is common, deep-rooted, and deadly—at least to your productivity.

Workloads Are Fierce

If you think you have too much to do, you might be right. Many professionals today do the work of one-and-a-half or two people. Corporate downsizing, once last-resort, has become business-as-usual. Companies expect everyone to do more with less. Small business owners carry an especially great burden, playing multiple roles outside their skill sets.

Improved technology picks up some of the slack, but it adds to the strain as well. Computers and smart phones enable us to accomplish some tasks more quickly than ever, but they also generate more to do, see, and read—all at our fingertips. As a result, we face too many choices, opportunities, and expectations. Too much to do, period.

Whether you are an attorney, CEO, financial advisor, executive, small business owner, or manager, your situation is probably the same. You look pulled together, but behind closed doors you

21: I CAN DO IT ALL MYTH

scramble to keep up. You try to answer every email and voice mail promptly. Follow up on every opportunity. Bring every idea to fruition. Do everything you are asked. How is that going?

The American Dream and Reality

We Americans like to believe we can accomplish whatever we set our minds to do. We learn this idea as children—if you can dream it, you can do it. It is debatable whether that notion was ever true but today it is not. The media offers so many possibilities, it is physically impossible to achieve all the dreams you can dream.

Here is the stark reality: you cannot read all the books, magazines, and electronic updates you want to read, much less write all the books, articles, and blogs you want to write. You cannot watch all the travel shows you enjoy, much less visit all the places they feature. You cannot see all the movies, participate in all the sports, compete in all the competitions, or pursue all the hobbies you enjoy. You cannot stay connected with all the people who want to be your online friends and spend all the quality time with your family that you think you should. It really is too much.

> You will never get fully caught up. You will never get it all done. And that's a good thing.

Neta, a psychotherapist, knows this firsthand. "I think the myth that you can do it all is a pervasive one, especially among Type A, high-performing people. Breaking through that myth is an ongoing process," she says.

"I Can Get Caught Up Someday" Fiction

The "I can do it all" myth persists in part because of the "I can get caught up someday" fiction that fuels it. Most people fall prey to it at some point. You want to get your work "done" in such a way that you will not fall behind again. "If only I could come in over the weekend," you think. "If only I could just have a week with no interruptions." "If only things would slow down for just a while." "If only..."

In fact, you **can** get through that pile of backlogged tasks if you come in on the weekend. And then the deluge starts again Monday. In truth, you will never get fully caught up. You will never get it all done. And that's a good thing.

THE PRODUCTIVITY CHAIN

Today's "knowledge work" flows like a river. As you watch a stream, the individual water molecules speed past you, ever-changing, yet the water level remains constant. That's how your work flows, too. Complete one case, one project, one file, one deal, and another takes its place. If it did not, you would need to re-fill your pipeline fast—and that's just another new project. The work never ends.

Dangerous Delusion

Aside from exhausting you, the myth that you can do it all fools you into making poor decisions about how to spend your time *now*. This dangerous delusion prevents you from giving your work the brutal triage it deserves.

In crisis situations, medical professionals must determine quickly and ruthlessly who to treat, who can wait, and who will be left to die. This rapid, reality-based decision-making is called triage. In the ongoing crisis of work overload, you need to approach your projects, tasks, and ideas the same way.

> If you truly accepted that you could not do it all, you would be more careful about the commitments you make.

If you truly accepted that you could not do it all, you would be much more careful about which commitments you make. You would say "no" to the many low-return activities swelling your to-do list. You would make the difficult decisions to drop that project, change the scope of another, pursue this prospect but not the other, and so on.

Believing the "do it all" myth lets you avoid the painful decisions. It makes you spread yourself too thin and even waste time. But avoiding decisions *is* a decision—a decision to let Fate, circumstances, or other people decide what you do or don't do. You give up your power this way.

You are like a skilled juggler with too many pins to handle. You can pick which ones to set aside to juggle later or never—this is triage. Or you can try to juggle them all and watch as some crash to the ground. Some *will* crash—usually important ones, such as your personal life or that lucrative idea you forgot to write down. Your peace of mind usually crashes, too. Trying to do it all causes disappointment, guilt, and a sense of inadequacy when you find you can't.

21: I CAN DO IT ALL MYTH

The Productivity Chain Solution: Practice Humility

"It was just the realization that I couldn't do it all. There are just not enough hours in the day."
  –Carleen, graphic designer

The only blade that can pierce the "do-it-all" delusion is humility. It may seem a strange word to find in a business book, but it belongs. Humility means accepting your human limitations. Since you cannot do it all, you must wisely choose what you **will** do.

You practice humility by saying "no" or "not now" to yourself and others. You practice it by taking items off your to-do list—even good ideas that just don't make the cut. You practice it by letting yourself rest. The stronger your Boundary-setting and Decision-making links, the better you can practice humility (and vice versa).

It is popular nowadays to think you must be available for work twenty-four hours a day, seven days a week. When you examine the kind of work done after hours, on weekends, and before breakfast, however, it usually turns out to be routine matters that could be handled during the day (and sometimes by someone else).

You may like to get these tasks out of the way so you can handle **other** matters during business hours. But sacrificing your "free" time depletes your energy for the next day. Instead, focus solely on your most important work while you are at work, letting lower priority matters drop. Your productivity will improve, guaranteed. It just takes some humility.

Brandon's Story

Brandon, a technology consultant, discovered that humility improved his relationships, customer service, and bottom line. He sought my help so he could spend more time—or better quality time—with his family. His wife complained that he was always on the phone when at home, working. He agreed that he needed to strengthen his Health link.

When advised to limit his phone use after a certain hour, however, he resisted. Brandon thought his constant availability set him apart from his competitors. What if there were an emergency? These "do it all" thoughts weakened his Boundary-setting link.

THE PRODUCTIVITY CHAIN

One incident finally changed his mind. A needy client contacted him with a problem one evening. Brandon made several calls over the next hours, trying to fix the situation. Later, he learned the client had found a solution on his own. If Brandon had not checked his email until the morning, he would have learned a problem had been identified and solved without his involvement. Instead, he jumped through hoops and neglected his family for nothing. This experience was not new. It was just the last straw.

He humbly accepted he was not the solution to everyone's problems. He couldn't "do it all" for his clients or his family—and certainly not for both. He started to put his phone on the dresser in the evenings so he would not be tempted to check it compulsively.

At first, Brandon felt anxious when 8:00 PM rolled around and he had to let go of his device. After a couple weeks, though, his concern decreased. Eventually, without prompting, he began putting his phone in a drawer, not even checking his emails before bed, as he had done previously.

In the inevitable way that strengthening one link leads to strengthening another (the Chain Reaction described in Chapter 2: *How the Productivity Chain Functions*), Brandon became aware of how his phone use interfered with his client meetings. He couldn't give his full attention to the person in front of him, and he followed up poorly with the caller because he couldn't take notes or make thoughtful decisions. He decided to silence his phone during meetings, improving his Communication/Relationships link and his connection with clients.

> **Brandon became aware of how his phone use interfered with his client meetings.**

Brandon's boundaries with technology—and therefore some people—led him to rely more on his support staff to serve some of his customers. (His Delegation link improved.) He could then concentrate on his top clients and prospects, giving them better care than before.

Did humility make Brandon less effective? Hardly. At year's end, he won a national award for revenue generation. On a daily basis, he was more focused and effective. Best of all, his wife and child loved having his full attention when he was home—his original reason for changing.

21: I CAN DO IT ALL MYTH

By accepting that he couldn't do it all, Brandon actually accomplished more than ever.

Myth:	**I can do it all.**
Reality:	I have to choose what matters most.
Harm Caused by Myth:	It prevents me from making important decisions, so I mis-use my time.
PC Solution:	Practice humility when it comes to commitments and availability.
Link(s) to Strengthen:	Boundary-setting, Decision-making

Myth 22   I Need More Time

> "My problem is time—the lack of it. With work, children, and a husband, I'm swamped. I never get a break."
> —Tina, electrical engineer

You may think, as Tina does, that you just need more time to solve your productivity problem. Many people share this belief. Yet, when you try to solve "lack of time" by spending more time at work, it doesn't help. Why? Because time isn't the problem and it isn't the solution.

Time Isn't the Problem

We humans have all the time we need to accomplish great things.

We have just as many hours in a day as Mozart and Einstein, Bill Gates and Warren Buffett. We have the same amount of time as Henry Ford, Mother Teresa, Martin Luther, Martin Luther King, Jr., Stephen King, Stephen Hawking, Oprah Winfrey, Mahatma Gandhi, Cleopatra, and every world leader—past, present, and future.

Time itself is not the limiting factor. It's what we **do** with our time that matters. It is a subtle, yet crucial distinction. Some people use their time well. Most do not.

Defining *time* as the problem—the reason we can't achieve our goals—is not accurate or helpful. It creates a subtle sense of helplessness and hopelessness because you can't control time. If time is your problem, then you are stuck, as "New Labels, New Solutions" in Chapter 3: *A Powerful Perspective* points out. The reality, however, is very different.

> *To say 'I don't have time' is to say 'I don't want to.'*
> Lao Tzu

22: I NEED MORE TIME MYTH

Time Isn't the Solution, Either

If you think lack of time is your problem, it makes sense to solve it by throwing more time at the situation. That's what many Americans do. U.S. workers put in more hours than most of our industrialized nations' counterparts. We work nine forty-hour weeks a year more than the Germans, for instance, and they still out-produce us.[1] We also sleep less than we need, skip lunch, and forfeit vacation time. We stay late at the office and work on weekends. While at home, we remain connected to work via phone, email, and texts.

> There are limited hours in the day and a limitless number of things you could do. Even a hundred-hour day is not enough.

Of course, throwing time at the problem like this **can** help in the short term. It is perfect for the occasional crisis or caffeine-fueled all-nighter in college. It is **not** effective in the long run.

Why More Time Doesn't Help

Solving "lack of time" with more time fails for several reasons:

- **Limited Time:** There are limited hours in the day and a limitless number of things you could do. Even a hundred-hour day would not be not enough. Working longer hours to get it all done is like managing your debt by extending your credit limit. The hole just deepens.

- **Law of Diminishing Returns:** If you regularly work too much, you accomplish less in a given hour than you could otherwise. Your energy decreases, your thinking dulls, and you make more mistakes. You don't even realize it because tiredness impairs your ability to judge whether you are impaired.

- **Needs and Values Conflict:** Too much time at work often conflicts with your personal needs and values. If you believe "family comes first," you feel torn when you put work first again and again. If you need music, nature, travel, woodworking—or whatever—to be happy, yet rarely meet that need, you feel dissatisfied. When you continually disregard your needs and values, your soul withers. Eventually, your motivation for work withers, too.

THE PRODUCTIVITY CHAIN

- **Less Time Working:** When you chronically overwork, you may spend less time actually working. Your sense of urgency diminishes and you spend more time socializing or doing personal business, which forces you to spend more time at your desk, whether you want to or not.

It's wonderful to work all the time if work is your pleasure. But even then, you need to rest sometimes. As humans, we need to completely detach from work to recharge our batteries, however much we love and value our jobs—and especially when we don't love them so much. Longer hours eventually worsen the "not enough time" situation. (See Chapter 23: *I Need to Work Harder*.)

The Productivity Chain Solution: A "Just Enough" Time Mindset

What improves your situation? Believing you have "just enough" time to do what matters—*if* you use it wisely. That belief alone changes your mindset—strengthening your Drive link. You go from scarcity to abundance, from powerless to powerful. You feel calmer. You don't bite off more than you can chew. And you don't feel deprived at the things you "miss" because your time matches your needs and values.

Ava's Story

Ava, an experienced private banker, changed her thinking from "not enough" to "just enough" time and it paid off in more deposits. Her former prospecting strategy left her exhausted and short of her goals for two reasons. First, she tried to make too many prospecting calls and visits per week. Second, she spent too much time pursuing certain prospects. They had huge portfolios but no interest in changing banks at present.

Ava's Productivity Chain Self-Assessment made her realize her Planning, Goal-setting/Prioritization, and Drive links were weak—the true cause of her failure to achieve her goals.

She began to practice "just enough" time by limiting and actually scheduling her prospecting calls. Her days became more manageable and she felt successful when she met her "quota." She

22: I NEED MORE TIME MYTH

actually called more people than before because her endless list had been so overwhelming, she sometimes avoided it.

The "just enough" limit forced her to make tough decisions about which people to target. She reluctantly let go of those "big fish" and found, to her surprise, that she immediately felt lighter and more energized. She stopped dreading those calls; her Drive link got a boost.

When she stopped pouring time into unlikely prospects, she had plenty of time for those who wanted her business. She soon landed several accounts almost as large as the "big fish" she had cut. She reached her annual target numbers well before the deadline—a first.

> *Those who make the worst use of their time are the first to complain of its shortness.*
> Jean de la Bruysre

When you accept that your time is limited, you realize you have just enough—and only enough—time for what you truly need to accomplish. As Wesley, a film producer, says, "It's a paradox. We really have no control over time, in terms of mortality, but in another sense, we very much have control over how we spend it. Use the fact that you can't control the one to make you want to control the other more." His words underscore the reality that time is not our problem, nor our solution. It is what we **do** with our time that matters.

Myth:	**I need more time.**
Reality:	I have all the time I need.
Harm Caused by Myth:	I use my time poorly and experience diminishing returns.
PC Solution:	Prioritize what I will do with my "just enough" time.
Link(s) to Strengthen:	Drive

Myth 23  I Need to Work Harder

"I value my work ethic. I'm trying to teach my children that no matter what you do, work at it hard. But the older I get, the more I want better results in less time. I want to work smarter, more strategically—not just work, work, work."
—Tony, manager of budget analysts

Commonsense says you would accomplish more if you just got busy and worked harder. If throwing more time at the problem of "too much to do" does not solve it, maybe more effort and speed will.

It's worked so far—sort of. You have a good career. You accomplish a great deal, although you know you could achieve more. You do not stop from that first email in the morning until your last call at night. You are always busy—why isn't that enough to make you happy with your productivity, or with your personal life, or both?

"Busy-ness" may actually keep you from the life you want. You can be too busy—too busy to decide what is important, too busy to change, even too busy to do the work that produces the most results. You may be busy ***doing***, but not always ***producing***.

The idea that working harder and being busy-er will improve productivity is a myth. It's a twin to the myth that getting more organized will solve all your problems (Chapter 24). In reality, your effort must be spent on the ***right*** activities to be effective. Some people do need to work harder, but even then, putting the nose to the grindstone only helps if it's the right grindstone.

Misdirected activity, on the other hand, hurts you and the bottom line—wasting time, energy, and resources. "Muscling" through your work leaves you exhausted, sometimes with little to

23: I NEED TO WORK HARDER MYTH

show for it. As Linda, a web designer, explains, "There are people I know who have a tremendous work ethic. They work very hard yet, at the end of a given year or quarter, they have not been that productive because it was not [properly] focused activity."

> *It's not enough to be busy. The question is: what are we busy about?*
> — Henry David Thoreau

A strong work ethic is a good and necessary thing. Approaching your duties with focus, effort, energy, and enthusiasm is an important link in the Productivity Chain (Drive link). But it must be directed towards the right target or it becomes mere busy-ness.

"Busy" Does Not Mean "Productive"

"Since I started being more productive, I realize I used to think that just being busy was being productive. Now I see a lot of stuff we do is a waste of time. Being productive is being smart with your time."
—Jo, product manager, medical device manufacturer

Like "organized," "busy" doesn't mean "productive." How can you distinguish the two? Here are a few ways:

- When you are productive, you accomplish your most important tasks. Achievement matters more than effort. When you are merely busy, you do lots of work—any work, no matter how urgent, important, or necessary.

- When you are productive, work flows through your office like a stream: it goes in and comes out. When you are merely busy, your office becomes a swamp where significant projects get backed up while you work on other matters.

- When you are productive, you prioritize your tasks according to their importance. When you are just busy, you prioritize by the ease with which you can check an item off your list.

If you have been more busy than productive lately, have no shame. Everyone has been, at times. If you do it regularly, though, it can stall your motivation and your career. "Working hard without an objective in mind, without some thought of where you want your work to lead, puts you on an endless treadmill," says Crystal, a solo entrepreneur. That treadmill is pretty crowded.

THE PRODUCTIVITY CHAIN

Working Harder Makes You Busy-er

The reasons for busy-ness vary. Whatever its origins, unchecked busy-ness impairs other links in the Productivity Chain—forcing you to work still harder to be productive, worsening the problem.

- **Bad Habit:** Busy-ness becomes a habit and, for some, an addiction—a behavior they feel compelled to do even when its costs outweigh its benefits. Workaholics Anonymous notes that workaholics rely on their tasks for self-worth—and they can never do enough.[2] They may "win" recognition and advancement, but lose their families and themselves in the process. Their Drive link impairs their other links.

- **Trouble at Home:** Constant busy-ness creates a vicious circle between home and work. Too much time at the office leads to disharmony with loved ones or a sense of emptiness. That unhappiness leads to avoidance through work, which leads to still greater tension or loneliness.

    RJ, the management consultant, has witnessed this phenomenon many times. "It's a real issue," he says. "When we've gone deep with some clients, we've discovered they don't want to go home for valid reasons. It's not good at home." Whether that is a cause or an effect of the overworking doesn't matter. Their Health link is weak.

- **Avoidance:** For many, busy-ness is a procrastination device. Important projects are often difficult and unfamiliar; it's easier to do routine matters instead. "I haven't started projects X, Y, or Z, but I've answered all my calls and emails, even the irrelevant ones," Tina, an engineer, admitted during her assessment. Procrastination indicates a weak Drive link.

- **Fire-fighting:** Poor planning creates little "fires," another source of busy-ness. It's the kitty litter syndrome. When you don't clean the litter daily, waste builds up. Your cat, disgusted by the inattention, takes her business elsewhere, creating a costly, time-consuming, and utterly preventable "fire."

    Multiply this scenario by twenty projects and substitute "client" for "cat," and you become a part-time firefighter, which reflects weak Goal-setting/Prioritization and Planning links.

23: I NEED TO WORK HARDER MYTH

- **Over-commitment:** Taking on too many tasks and obligations causes busy-ness. Few people like to say "no" to others or themselves, so they don't. Instead, they become people-pleasers, who end up pleasing no one as work slips through the cracks and deadlines pass by, unmet. Over-commitment occurs when the Boundary-setting link is weak.
- **Over-stimulation:** Like exhausted toddlers who run around ever more frantically, some people do not know when to quit. The less they sleep, the poorer their judgment. They stay busy, but increasingly less productive. Their Health link is too weak.

Busy-ness cannot last forever. Eventually, you face burnout and even illness. Before that happens, you may tarnish your reputation by becoming the Don't-Go-To person in the office.

These are good reasons to get off the treadmill now. But there is an even better reason: you do not want to work so hard that you miss your own life.

The Productivity Chain Solution: Work Smarter, Not Harder

As with all productivity myths, you can practice the 3A's—Awareness, Acceptance, and Action—to let go of the mistaken belief that hard work alone will make you more productive. When this myth no longer blinds you, you can assess yourself or your situation using the Productivity Chain. (See Chapter 20: *Overcome Your Productivity Myths* and Chapter 4: *Identify Solutions*.)

Your Productivity Chain Analysis will direct you to strengthen specific links, which enables you to "work smarter, not harder." Working smarter means working on your most important tasks—the ones that produce the most significant results.

Applying the Pareto Principle helps. When you focus your effort on the 20 percent of activities that produce 80 percent of the desired results, you don't have to waste time on the 80 percent that produce the 20 percent of results. (It's not always 80/20, of course, but the principle applies.)

Your Goal-setting/Prioritization link will probably be one you will need to strengthen, since one characteristic of busy-ness is lack

THE PRODUCTIVITY CHAIN

of, or ineffective, prioritizing. Your Boundary-setting link may need attention, as well. To work smarter, you have to say "no" to activities that are comfortable, enjoyable, and even somewhat productive, so you can concentrate on those that are **most** productive.

Saying "no" to yourself can be difficult, but self-discipline makes it possible. Working too hard is an example of the *effort* aspect of your Drive link going into hyper-drive. Discipline, part of the *attitude* facet of your Drive, enables you to correct course.

Discipline is a commitment to habits and practices—in this case the practice of boundary-setting and prioritizing. Like your links, your discipline will grow ever stronger with use. (For practical strategies to strengthen those weak links, see Chapter 8: ***Boundary-setting*** and Chapter 13: *Goal-setting/Prioritization*.)

Myth:	**I need to work harder.**
Reality:	Activity is not productivity; busy-ness is a problem in itself.
Harm Caused by Myth:	I lose perspective about the difference between productivity and busy-ness and feel defeated when I don't produce.
PC Solution:	Use discipline to work smarter, not harder.
Link(s) to Strengthen:	Boundary-setting, Drive, Goal-setting/Prioritization

Myth

 **I Need to Get More Organized**

"Even though my desk is messier, I'm more productive."
—Caleb, marketing consultant

People say "I need to be more organized" all the time. They think it will solve their problems, help them accomplish what they want, and feel more in control. As one workshop participant recently told me, "Getting organized is my lifelong mission."

As a Certified Professional Organizer,® this faith in organizing should be music to my ears. It's the reason the industry has expanded. Membership in the National Association of Productivity and Organizing Professionals (NAPO) has risen from a few people in 1983 to 3,500 in 2019.[3] As a Productivity Coach, however, I know the limits of being organized—that's why I wrote this book.

Although they think getting organized will solve their productivity problems, many of my clients are well-organized people when it comes to their objects and information. They have little clutter on or in their desks or computers. They automatically think in terms of categorizing, retrieving, and simplifying.

Still, Gretchen often missed deadlines she set and marked on her color-coded calendar. Gail didn't accomplish the most important tasks on her perfectly formatted to-do list. And Ethan's ability to retrieve a file in fifteen seconds or less mattered little when he woke up at 3:00 AM, worrying about work.

They hire me because they know something is missing. Soon, they learn that Organization of Objects/Data is just one link in their Productivity Chains. The "something missing" that they seek is usually **another** link—or three. For them, getting more organized was like drinking cold medicine for an upset stomach. It couldn't cure what ailed them.

What Does "Organize" Mean?

To "organize" means to put something in order,[4] which is fairly broad. As noted before, people use the word in many contexts. It can mean clearing clutter in an attic, managing time, improving your marriage, or getting out of debt. As a result, the word is not specific enough to be useful.

As a link in the Chain, "organization" refers to the organization of objects and data, both physical and electronic. It enables you to access information and tools rapidly. This narrower definition allows you to easily assess your proficiency in this area. If it's high, you can look at other links for the solutions you need. If it's low, see Chapter 15: *Organization of Objects/Data* for suggestions about how to strengthen that link.

Organized Enough to Rake Leaves?

I once heard someone say, "You have to be organized to rake leaves"—a typical "organizing" remark. But is that true? In reality, raking leaves requires **just enough** Organization of Objects/Data to grab your rake. That's a pretty low threshold. The actual raking requires a decision to do it (Decision-making link), the time set aside to do it (Planning link), and the execution of it (Drive and Task/Project Management links).

If your leaves remain on the ground and you know where your rake is and can reach it, disorganization has nothing to do with your lack of productivity in the yard. In the same way, piles on your desk may have nothing to do with your organizing knowledge, skills, and abilities.

These fine distinctions are crucial when it comes to work performance. We need specific, targeted solutions to our productivity problems and "organization" is too broad a brush with which to paint. The Productivity Chain helps you assess what's really going on.

When Getting More Organized Can Help

A weak Organization of Objects/Data link can damage your productivity, of course. Bill, a government contractor, frequently had to re-do work he misplaced. Evelyn, a realtor, couldn't list a

24: I NEED TO GET MORE ORGANIZED MYTH

multi-million-dollar beach property because she lost the prospect's business card and could not recall his name. These losses are real.

If you often spend large amounts of time looking for things (e.g., keys, papers, or digital files) or you have recurring difficulty managing information and ideas, getting more organized ***can*** increase your productivity. All those hours spent searching can be spent on other activities. The quality of your work product may even improve.

And you save time and money when you do not have to re-do documents, re-check work, or re-purchase items. These are the fruits of better-organized objects and data.

When Getting More Organized Can Hurt

For many people, however, getting more organized will not substantially increase productivity because it frees only a small portion of time. The clutter they accumulate is a ***symptom*** of how they spend their time, rather than a root cause of their struggles.

If they weren't so over-committed or if they delegated more, for example, they would have time to put things away. They know how and where. Their Organization of Objects/Data link is temporarily weak only because they are not applying it.

This was the case for Carol, the corporate vice president from page 1. She found that addressing her genuinely weak links made it relatively easy for her to get her objects and data back into shape.

> *The trouble with organizing a thing is that pretty soon folks get to paying more attention to the organization than to what they're organized for.*
>
> Laura Ingalls Wilder

Still, many people perceive a neat and orderly space as evidence of productivity. "A cluttered environment conveys waste and sloth and procrastination," is how one client put it. To avoid that appearance, people strive to get more organized. These efforts can backfire.

How "Organizing" Can Waste Time

Here are some ways "getting organized" can be counterproductive and time-wasting.

- **"Procrastination by Organization:"** You can easily spend more time organizing and preparing your work than actually doing it. Paula, a paralegal, could not start any project until she cleared her desk of all papers, even if the "clutter" were low-priority and not in her way. Her file folders were crisp, with matching labels, and she liked to create sharp-looking binders of reports that would never be opened again.

  "It's easy to get caught up in these little organizational tasks that feel productive and are very easy to hide behind. But the tough thing is getting on the phone and making that call, or getting prepared for that meeting, or having that meeting," reports Tom, a healthcare executive. "If you're not doing that, then all the organization in the world won't do you any good."

- **Unnecessary Fixes:** Many successful, intelligent people want to be even more effective, so they purchase any product or service related to "organizing." When that link in their Chain is already sufficiently strong, their time and money is wasted. Meanwhile, they don't address their true productivity problems.

- **Unrealistic Demands:** The cultural focus on "organization" feeds some people's drive for perfection and overachievement. A group of female professionals who once asked me to share tips on organizing their things illustrates this point.

  It became clear that what these organized-enough women really needed was to ease up on themselves. No amount of containers or shelving was going to fix the "problem" of full-time, stressful careers, coupled with full-time household and familial responsibilities.

  The drive to get more organized just added unnecessary pressure to their lives. Instead of rearranging their closets, their time might be better spent changing their expectations, practicing self-acceptance, surrendering to a certain level of chaos, and taking some relaxing hot baths.

Some Very Successful People Are Disorganized

While some people pursue getting organized in ways that make them less productive and more stressed, others who are "organizationally challenged" do quite well—more evidence that

24: I NEED TO GET MORE ORGANIZED MYTH

"organized" doesn't mean "productive."

Kinko's founder Paul Orfalea,[5] author and marketing guru Seth Godin,[6] and economist Diane Swonk[7]—three highly successful professionals—have all publicly discussed having Attention Deficit Disorder (ADD), a condition whose diagnostic criteria actually includes being disorganized and losing things.

Some of my clients who have ADD are among the most accomplished in terms of career advancement, recognition, income, and esteem from colleagues. They are brilliant, creative, and incapable of maintaining order in their offices or computers without assistance (and sometimes even then).

Being disorganized does not hold them back. They may feel frustrated at times because they cannot meet the societal demand to "have it all together" and "look good" in that respect, but so what? Most of us fail to meet any number of societal demands, from being the "right" weight to having the "right" career. The social stigma about being disorganized obscures the fact that some people with messy desks accomplish a great deal.

While having a weak Organization of Objects/Data link may hamper them in some respects, they make sure it does not compromise their overall productivity. They make that link just strong enough or they actively coordinate with more-organized associates to prevent disorganization from getting in the way. (See Chapter 29: *Others Can Make Up for What I Lack* for more about striking that balance.)

In a productivity contest between a disorganized person who completes her most important tasks and an organized individual who evades his top-priority work, the disorganized person wins every time.

The Productivity Chain Solution:
See Organization as a Means, Not an End

If you have believed the myth that you need to get more organized when you really don't, you are not alone. To overcome it, try to see organization as a means to an end. Clarify what you really want to achieve—what you need to produce—and ask yourself whether organizing something ***now*** will help you achieve it.

THE PRODUCTIVITY CHAIN

If not, do a Productivity Chain Self-Assessment or Situation Analysis (Chapter 4: *Identify Solutions*) to see what your real weaknesses are, and what solutions would benefit you most.

Practicing self-acceptance helps this process. When you lower your expectations and tolerate, even welcome, a small amount of chaos into your world, you free your energy to spend time in ways that matter most to you.

And if you enjoy the process of getting organized so much that you find it difficult to stop, accept that, too. Consider it a hobby and do it in your spare time. Or make it a profession. But don't confuse it with productivity!

Myth:	**I need to get more organized.**
Reality:	Being organized is just one link in the Productivity Chain—and it might not be my weak link.
Harm Caused by Myth:	I waste time trying to fix what isn't broken and can get sucked into perfectionism.
PC Solution:	See getting organized as a means to an end and practice self-acceptance.
Link(s) to Strengthen:	Depends on my Productivity Chain Analysis

Myth 25: I Should Be Able to Handle Everything Myself

"I used to be on more on top of things. I had a better memory. Of course, my business was smaller then and I didn't have kids..."
—RJ, management consultant

If you can relate to RJ's comment, you are not alone. Many people who used to be able to "handle" the details of their work gradually find their old systems fraying at the seams. They have too much to keep track of anymore.

The slide into unmanageability can be slow or abrupt. A birth, death, or some other life-changing event may tip the balance. The accumulated weight of greater responsibilities, age, tiredness, and distraction take their toll. Fundamentally, though, the problem is biological. We have dial-up brains in a broadband world.

Our Dark Age Brains

We still have essentially the same brains humans have always had, but today we need them to process so much more. As an average adult during the Dark Ages, for example, you would probably never stray past your village. You knew only your small circle of family and friends. You could not read and had no TV or computer.

Your options—from profession to spouse—were limited or nonexistent. Daily decisions about your time and tasks were simpler, too. Your work involved manual labor and you didn't have a watch. When daylight faded, your work faded, too.

> We have dial-up brains in a broadband world.

Fast-forward to today. As the familiar statistic goes, you will find more words in one day's *New York Times* than most people saw in their lives back then. Information hurls at you from every direction by computers, phones, TVs, radios, billboards, T-shirts, books, magazines, mail, movies, and cereal boxes.

Your life options seem boundless. You can change careers, go to school, move to a different country, marry someone you love. Your only limits are resources, drive, desire—and your human body.

Our Dark Age brains try to handle all the stimulation and options. Like computers from the 1980s with limited storage and slow speeds, however, they can only process and remember so much. They, too, can lock up. Memory training helps only a bit. Even people who have eidetic memory—perfect recall of what they see, read, or hear—can find work unmanageable. (I've had a couple of them as clients.)

The Productivity Chain Solution: Stop Trying to Handle It

So how can you be productive without running yourself into the ground? Strange as it seems, you give up. If you can't manage it on your own brain power, stop trying. Some define "insanity" as doing the same behavior over and over, expecting different results. That's what you may have been doing with your work.

It is a myth that you should be able to handle everything yourself. The reality is you can't. No one can. So stop "should"-ing on yourself. You are not defective. You haven't "lost it." Your responsibilities have simply outgrown your brain's capacity to cope. Accepting this human limitation frees you to get support:

- **Get an "external hard drive" for your brain.** Project lists, task lists, checklists, calendared appointments, and reminders provide the support your brain needs. They're like an external hard drive. Find strategies that work for you and commit to them. In other words, strengthen your Task/Project Management and Planning links.

- **Ask for help.** Assign projects or parts of projects whenever possible. Let go of entire roles or responsibilities if you can, so you only (or mostly) handle work with the greatest value to the organization. Have your assistant keep your calendar—and you—on track. Work on your Delegation link.

25: I SHOULD BE ABLE TO HANDLE EVERYTHING MYTH

Jing Song, a commercial architect, used his computer only for his drawings and research. His assistant handled his email, appointments, and administrative matters. They met daily, had clear guidelines for what matters she needed to clear with him, and he trusted her judgment on the rest. As a result, he could really focus on his work and his clients. He especially enjoyed the mental clarity he found when he used email only rarely.

You might also do the "Compare Your Golden Age with Today" exercise (Chapter 32: *The Problem Will Get Better by Itself*) to understand what has changed since you used to "handle it all," just as a reality check.

Myth:	**I should be able to handle everything myself.**
Reality:	I have human limitations and need support.
Harm Caused by Myth:	Feeling like a failure.
PC Solution:	Stop trying to handle it all and rely on external support—from lists to people.
Link(s) to Strengthen:	Delegation, Planning, Task/Project Management

Myth 26

I Can Make Up for Lost Time

"You don't have a work life and a social life. You have a life."
—Darryl, CEO, technology firm

"Time is money," they say. It's true that the faster you work, the more you can sell or bill. When you waste time, it translates into hard dollars or opportunity losses—the missed prospects or deals that might have brought in future revenue. Measured in these terms, time really is valuable.

But time is actually much more precious than money. It is your life.

In the rush of daily activities, it's easy to lose sight of this fact. You may think, as many do, that you will compensate for today's busyness later on. You'll sit and relax with your spouse once the deal is done. You'll go on that trip when you have a second-in-command trained, in a year or two. You'll start on that project tomorrow.

Believing you can make up for lost time is a myth that fuels many people's decisions. But this belief is where the time/money comparison breaks down. The reality is that while you can often make up for lost money, you can ***never*** make up for lost time. You can only resolve to spend your next moment more wisely.

> **TAKE ACTION**
> Take a moment or two to think about the fact that you only have so much time on this earth.

Similarly, you cannot save or grow time, the way you save money and watch it grow with interest. On a Friday, you can't stop at a bank to retrieve the extra hour you deposited there earlier that week. You can only spend time—wisely or not. You know all this intellectually, but applying that knowledge takes practice.

26: I CAN MAKE UP FOR LOST TIME MYTH

Think About It...Really Hard

It may sound trite to say you only have so much time on this earth, but it is true. You hear it so often you probably don't really think about it. Think about it now.

That's what Max, an executive in a construction firm, did. It prompted him to make significant changes in his approach to work. "I couldn't physically do it all in a day and have a family life," he explains. "What happened before was that the family suffered. That's where my 'free' time [to work longer hours] came. I knew I couldn't continue on that path. It's no life for them to always see their dad at work. I didn't want to be that kind of dad or husband."

We humans have just enough time for our needs—**and no more**. (See Chapter 22: *I Need More Time* for more about "just enough" time.) To make your personal and professional plans and goals realistic, you have to accept that your time is finite.

Time is not a mesh bag that stretches to fit whatever you stuff in it. An hour is like a sturdy wooden box with a lid. It can accommodate only so many activities—so put your most important ones in first.

> An hour is a wooden box with a lid, not a mesh bag that stretches.

Of course, during some hours you can accomplish more than in others. When you are awake, you achieve more than when you are asleep (or at least what you achieve is more visible and valued). When you are well-fed, well-rested, highly motivated, mentally engaged, and uninterrupted, you do more in an hour than you would in opposite conditions. Nevertheless, at some point there is only so much that you can cram into a sixty-minute stretch and, by extension, into a lifetime.

How Much Time Do You Have?

Analyzing how many hours you have at your disposal during a given day or week can be useful. Embracing the reality of time and its constraints is the first step in changing how you use your time. The "Raise Your Time Awareness" exercise on the next page can serve as your guide.

Just becoming more aware of how you spend your time creates the opportunity to cut waste. Giving up or reducing TV, internet, or

THE PRODUCTIVITY CHAIN

> **Exercise: Raise Your Time Awareness**
>
> Writing down your activities and commitments helps you appreciate how much time you really have on a given day. If you fall into "magical thinking" about time, this exercise can bring you back to reality. If you already have a good sense of time, it may help you plan even better. You can do the same analysis of your activities while at work, as well.
>
> - **The 24 hours of a typical work day.** Write down how much time you spend: working, commuting, sleeping, eating, preparing and cleaning up after meals, physically caring for children or others, and grooming (morning and evening). How much time is left?
>
> - **The 24 hours of a typical weekend day.** Write down how much time you spend: grocery-shopping, doing other required shopping, running errands, physically caring for children or others, house cleaning and maintaining, doing yard work, and handling personal finances. How much time is left?
>
> - **What's left.** Write down what's missing from the lists above, e.g., relaxed time with your loved ones, exercise, personal development, and so on, and how much time you spend on each.
>
> How does your use of time align with your values and needs?

video games, for example, opens up a lot of time for most Americans. It also makes you feel less stressed and influenced by the consumption-driven culture that those devices promote.

Letting go of resentments, worrying, and doing for others what they could do for themselves also frees up time for many. Other options to consider include working from home, preparing meals in advance, outsourcing, and simplifying. The list could go on.

Once you see how limited your "just enough" time is, you might even be inspired to create the life you really want (if you have not already). It's a life that fits who you are and what you need. How would you spend your limited time then? If you feel unsure, think about the legacy you want to leave behind. Think, too, about your dreams and passions.

The clearer you are about what you want for your life, the more easily you can shape your time to create it.

26: I CAN MAKE UP FOR LOST TIME MYTH

What If You Want to Work More?

If your dreams revolve around your work, then you are blessed. If work gives transcendent meaning to your life, you will understandably want to spend as much time as possible doing it. Keep monitoring your Productivity Chain, in that case, so you can become and remain as effective and productive as possible.

If your work does not matter more than your personal life, however, you might want to consider how much time and energy you devote towards it. This is not a recommendation to goof off or quit. But if you work long hours consistently, evaluate whether you get a worthy return for the extra time you invest. You may.

If you don't, however, you have many options. You might start with the simplest and least disruptive: Strengthen the weaker links in your Productivity Chain so you can produce more results in less time. Then spend those freed-up hours on your passion—be it family, charity work, or model plane building.

The Productivity Chain Solution: Align Your Time with Your Values

To stop believing the "I can make up for lost time" myth, embrace the reality that time lost is life lost. You can then make more conscious decisions about how to spend your time. After you become aware of how precious your time is and accept how limited it is, take action to strengthen your weak links. Your Goal-setting/Prioritization link, in particular, must be strong enough to help you clarify, if you hadn't already, what you value most.

Your stronger Chain will then enable you to spend your time in ways that more closely align with your values, as Caleb and Chelsee did.

Caleb's Story

Caleb, a marketing consultant, committed to being at home by 3:00 PM when his children got off the school bus. He realized he would never be able to make up for time lost with his kids. In just a few years, they would leave home. He decided the best use of his time was to spend it with them.

THE PRODUCTIVITY CHAIN

To make it work, Caleb changed his job schedule, cutting his hours to thirty-five a week, down from forty or forty-five. He also started his work day earlier, letting his wife get the kids off to school. When possible, he used lunches for networking or client appreciation, so even "break" time was productive.

> When you think how a tight deadline forces you to take quick and decisive action, you know how Caleb felt most days.

A few months later, he was thrilled with the results. "I just don't do certain things anymore," Caleb says, explaining how he maintained his high productivity despite the new schedule. "And I don't let other things bother me. I don't have time to mess around."

His strong boundaries and sense of purpose created an urgency and pressure within him to perform more efficiently and wisely. He could then enjoy his family guilt-free and fully present mentally.

When you think how a tight deadline forces you to take quick and decisive action, you know how Caleb felt most days. That pressure required increased energy to sustain it, but he had that, too. "I feel so good about what I'm doing for my kids. They really need me and I am there for them. That gives me a lift every day," he explains.

Chelsee's Story

Chelsee, a primary care physician, believed strongly in military service. Her family had served in various branches for generations and she always thought she would spend her career there, too. She married young, however, and her husband persuaded her to remain a civilian, like him.

Years later, following their divorce, Chelsee felt that longing to serve her country rise again within her. She had a thriving practice with many patients and employees depending on her—the timing seemed all wrong. But Chelsee was fit, still relatively young, and single. She knew that she had to seize this opportunity because those factors would change later on.

Once she made the decision, everything fell into place. Chelsee got the best of both worlds. As a Naval officer in the reserves, she served part-time at a local Veterans Administration hospital. She also shared her private practice with another physician, working

26: I CAN MAKE UP FOR LOST TIME MYTH

two or three twelve-hour days a week there. She worked longer hours than she used to before but felt such fulfillment about her decision that she actually enjoyed her work more.

These are the stories of real people. You, too, can create the life you want. *Now* is the time to clarify your heart's longing. The more vividly you generate that image, the clearer your path becomes. When your values match your time, you tap into a reservoir of personal power that sustains and motivates you.

Myth:	I can make up for lost time.
Reality:	Time lost is life lost.
Harm Caused by Myth:	I miss out on my personal dreams.
PC Solution:	Clarify my dreams and use them to guide my decisions about time.
Link(s) to Strengthen:	Goal-setting/Prioritization

Myth 27

I Can't Play Until My Work Is Done

"You can have dessert after you eat your dinner."
   —Anonymous

I love scrapbooking. I do it digitally now, using software to create collages of images and text. The books arrive from the printer, bound and glossy-paged, like high school yearbooks but better. Every January, I begin a book for the previous year. Usually, I finish in April and take it on family visits.

Not this year. This year, I told myself I would finish the book you are reading. But I refused to cut back my client load. That work was more internally rewarding than writing, and it paid. And then my husband and I had this trip planned, and I got hired to speak at that event, and…Not surprisingly, progress on the book was slow. It was not a top priority.

In the evening and on weekends, I would think of scrapbooking. Then the guilt would strike: If I could scrapbook, I could work on ***this*** book. Since I did not want to work after putting in a full week, I would do neither.

I repeated this pattern more times than I like to admit before I finally remembered an old lesson: When I put my life on hold until all my work is done, I have no life. The work is **never** done. If I wait to play, I may never play.

Benefits and Costs of Delayed Gratification

Delaying gratification builds character. It is a hallmark of maturity. Usually, it is motivating, too. "I will eat the cookie after I run," you might think. Or "We'll tour Europe once the kids graduate." Or "I'll get a massage the day after tax season ends."

27: I CAN'T PLAY UNTIL MY WORK IS DONE MYTH

But the idea that work **must** always come first is another productivity myth, one especially prevalent in the United States, thanks to those pleasure-avoiding Puritans. My new clients express this myth frequently. It is the occupational equivalent of eating everything on your plate before getting dessert.

Most of us learned "I can't play until my work is done" as children. It helped us prioritize doing our homework before going out with friends. But homework was finite (regardless of how it felt). Your work is not. Still, if you could do what you need to do each day and just leave it all behind mentally, everything would be fine.

The problem occurs when you consistently postpone even small pleasures, such as relaxed time with family or self, hobbies, spiritual pursuits, or exercise, in favor of working or thinking about work. It becomes a problem when you put joy on hold until things "slow down" when experience says they never really slow down. How long can you delay the activities that bring pleasure, meaning, and value to your life? Only you can decide.

> It's a problem when you put joy on hold until things "slow down" and they never really slow down.

I decided when I found myself watching reruns to avoid "cheating" on my book writing with my scrapbooking. Life is too short for such nonsense. The reality is that I need to live fully today. A life delayed is a life less lived.

Once I remembered this hard-won truth, my mental stalemate ended. Days after I resumed the scrapbook, I began writing this book with renewed vigor, inspired to approach it from a more heartfelt perspective. Letting myself play made me more productive. Strengthening a weakened Health link always does.

The Productivity Chain Solution: Set Limits on Work

If you are postponing life's pleasures until all your work is done, you can free yourself, too. Since work always grows to fill the space allotted it, the solution lies in carving out time for the life you want and using those boundaries to contain your work. It requires, in other words, strong Boundary-setting and Planning links.

THE PRODUCTIVITY CHAIN

You don't have to take a sabbatical or plan an elaborate trip. You might begin by blocking out time on your calendar to exercise—and actually exercising then. You could commit to leaving work at a certain hour and stick to it. Or go swimming with your kids instead of doing the laundry. (Maybe they could help you wash clothes later.) And so on...

Kali's Story

It takes courage to set limits on work in a world that values work over play. Kali, an insurance executive, had that courage—and a strong Reinvention link. She wanted to maintain her career while pursuing her passion for world travel and deep-sea diving. After years of sixty-hour weeks, she craved a more fun and balanced life—and she didn't want to sacrifice her performance or income to get it. She realized that if she did not start that life now, she might be too injured or ill to enjoy it later.

She began by changing her mindset (Drive link). Instead of working hard so she could retire some day, she put her play first and viewed work as a means of financing it. Then, she scheduled her weeks of vacation throughout the year (Planning link). Suddenly, the timeframes for work projects became clear—and short.

As work contracted into periods of intense activity between trips, Kali's per-hour productivity actually increased. She found it easier to politely cut short the small talk and to manage her emails. Her focus and concentration improved. Because she made playing and enjoying life a top priority, her energy and attitude reached new highs, which helped her performance, as well.

When you stop waiting until you finish your work and begin living more fully now, you get the best of both worlds, as Kali did.

Myth:	I can't play until my work is done.
Reality:	I have to live fully now.
Harm Caused by Myth:	I postpone fulfillment while pursuing an impossible goal.
PC Solution:	Courage to set time limits on work.
Link(s) to Strengthen:	Boundary-setting, Health, Planning

Myth

I Am Not Naturally Productive

"I have to spend a lot of time thinking about how to manage my tasks. It doesn't come naturally for me, but that's not visible to other people."
—Crystal, solo entrepreneur

Some people seem to have arrived on this planet able to get things done. They appear to have a gene for hyper-productivity, making their work seem effortless. They instinctively bypass red tape, rarely waste time on trivial matters, have a well-developed sense of what is important, and the discipline to ignore all else. They usually have high physical energy. These people really do exist. They are uncommon—and uncommonly successful.

Then there are the rest of us.

You Are Still Growing

As Chapter 2: *How the Productivity Chain Functions*, explained, the links in most people's Productivity Chains vary widely in strength. Some links are solid steel, most are average, and a few could snap under pressure.

You may think that your productivity weaknesses are just "who you are"—as if your cake were fully baked. "I'm not good at that" or "I'm not naturally productive" secretly translates into "And that is how I will stay."

This myth—that since you weren't **born** hyper-productive, you can't **become** more productive—is a cop-out. There is no productivity gene. And you are not done baking. To believe you are denies your ability to change. It keeps you stuck.

The reality is that you are still learning and growing—whatever your age. The links in your Productivity Chain represent skills, knowledge, and abilities. Skills, like muscles, can be strengthened through persistent, challenging use. Knowledge can be obtained. Abilities can be developed.

Those uncommonly productive people don't have perfectly strong links; they just lack especially weak ones. When you practice new, more effective behaviors to strengthen your weak links, your overall productivity improves. You, too, can have a Power Chain, as they do. (See Chapter 6: *The Power Chain* for details.)

The Productivity Chain Solution: Stop Thinking "I'm Just Not Good at That!"

Before you can strengthen your Chain, you must be willing to let go of the mindset that you can't improve because "that's just how you are." You must, in other words, strengthen your Reinvention link. Usually, self-acceptance is a productivity asset, but when it comes to changing this false belief, it can get in your way.

How do you know whether "I'm just not good at that" is truth or excuse? Be honest with yourself. If you have **really** tried to develop a particular productivity skill, such as using a task list, and have made absolutely no progress despite many attempts and methods, and lots of practice, it might indeed be time to give up and accept your limitation. But such cases are rare.

Many people who "struggle" with productivity problems for decades actually make only sporadic and short-lived attempts to change. In fact, they "struggle" with handling the **consequences** of their current habits, not trying to develop new ones. They can't know whether they can succeed in changing or not, because they really haven't tried.

In the end, "I am just not good at that" is a negative mindset that weakens your Drive link and your willingness to change.

Productivity is learned.

The reality is that productivity requires learned behaviors. In a way, it's similar to singing. Singing is a skill, coupled with a little ability and knowledge. Just as most of us can walk, so most of us can sing. A few may be completely tone deaf. A few may have extraordinary instruments. The vast majority have average vocal cords and potential.

28: I AM NOT NATURALLY PRODUCTIVE MYTH

Most people fail to fulfill that potential. Because they believe they can't sing, they stop trying. Without practice, their vocal muscles weaken, their ears remain untrained, and, in time, they really can't sing. This is the definition of a self-fulfilling prophecy: the belief makes it so.

What is true for singing is true for productivity. While you might be that rare exception, "tone deaf" to planning or task/project management, for example, the odds are against it. It is more likely that your "muscles" in these areas just lack strength.

> You might have defined yourself (or been defined) at a young age as "disorganized" or "indecisive."

Why didn't those "muscles," those skills, develop early on? The same reason people stop singing. Maybe someone ridiculed them for it when they were young and impressionable. Maybe someone failed to show interest, so they stopped. Maybe no one in their family sang, so they internalized the belief that "we don't sing."

In much the same way, you might have defined yourself (or been defined) at a young age as "disorganized" or "indecisive." You might have thought "I don't plan ahead" or "I have to do everything myself" so often that those beliefs became into your reality.

Productivity takes practice.

Ultimately, "why" is irrelevant. What matters is "what now?" With training and effort, almost anyone can carry a tune. And with training and effort, anyone can improve their productivity. It "just" requires desire, commitment, humility, and consistent, repeated practice.

No one moves beyond potential into actualization without that practice. According to Malcolm Gladwell in *Outliers*, it takes at least 10,000 hours to become an expert in some area.[8] How many hours have you spent working on the weak links in your Productivity Chain?

The experience of the people in this book and others proves that even a few hours' effort can make a lasting improvement in your overall performance, if you exert the right kind of effort. After spending a few dozen hours on a given link, you will have started a new habit that may last for years.

Fortunately, you don't have to wait for 10,000 hours to pass

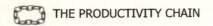
THE PRODUCTIVITY CHAIN

before you become a productivity powerhouse. And you don't need to be "naturally" productive, either.

Myth:	**I am not naturally productive.**
Reality:	I can learn productivity skills.
Harm Caused by Myth:	I may give up on myself and not try to change.
PC Solution:	Willingness and a positive mindset about change.
Link(s) to Strengthen:	Drive, Reinvention

Myth 29

Others Can Make Up for What I Lack

"I hate to say 'no' to people, so I don't. I tell them to call my assistant and she does it for me."
—*John, CEO of a conglomerate*

You may have always known the weak links in your Productivity Chain and hired others to compensate for them. If you are disorganized, for instance, a well-organized assistant can maintain and access the documents and information you need. If you lack tact, a spokesperson might carry your message to the people. If you are a visionary with no sense of the details, a Chief Operations Officer can bring your ideas to fruition.

You can and should hire people whose traits and skills complement your own. That is the advantage of working as part of a team. But even with their strengths around, you need to address your own weaknesses, at least enough to prevent them from undermining your team.

John, who runs several multi-million-dollar companies in his conglomerate, is learning this lesson. "I'm not good at follow-up," he admits. "I need people to do it for me." But when those people fall short—and they always seem to fall short—he's at a loss. Since he refuses to develop his own skills, he can't hold his staff accountable for theirs. He can't follow up on their follow-up.

Your Weak Links Affect Others' Chains, Too

John's dilemma reflects the myth that others can make up for what you lack. This false belief says you do not have to strengthen your weak links because you can rely on others' strong ones. The reality is that Productivity Chain principles apply to teams as well. A team

THE PRODUCTIVITY CHAIN

is only as strong as its weakest link (or member). The glaring shortcomings of one person—especially the leader—can undermine the strengths and performance of the whole group.

This undermining occurs in a couple of ways. First, your weak links directly affect those around you. If you have difficulty with Decision-making, for example, your team may waste time either waiting in limbo for your answer or scrapping work because you changed your mind. Their strengths don't matter at all.

Second, your weak link makes you delegate and run, as John did. You hand off some tasks, assuming (or hoping) you will never have to deal with it again. Unfortunately, that plan doesn't work because your people—however competent—need your involvement. Delegating and running indicates a weak Delegation link—a weakness created and sustained by the myth.

The "others can make up for what I lack" myth can be very difficult to admit having and, therefore, to let go. It usually operates below conscious awareness. Few people can admit they want others to assume their responsibilities. No one wants to believe they make unreasonable demands. Yet any supervisor can fall into the trap. And they often do. The consequences are particularly toxic because they harm others directly.

You Have to Participate

The reality is that your team cannot compensate *for* you; they compensate *with* you. As much as you may want them to read your mind and execute your plans, you have to communicate your ideas. You must be available for them—not always, but enough. Even if you explicitly ask them to manage you, you must **let** yourself be managed. "Delegate but participate," in other words.

Others can help you only to the extent that you cooperate with them. To see the value of your participation, imagine you have broken both legs and must be carried from bed to chair. At first, you go limp, not helping at all. Your aide must maneuver dead weight across the room—a difficult, if not impossible, task.

> Even if you explicitly ask others to manage you, you must let yourself be managed.

As he struggles, almost dropping you, you may understandably conclude he is weak, slow, or incompetent.

29: OTHERS CAN MAKE UP FOR WHAT I LACK MYTH

Now imagine you contract your muscles to carry some of your own weight and lean your body so your carrier can better support you. Your move occurs more quickly, easily, and pleasantly when you help him help you. You think he's pretty effective.

This analogy makes the need for your active participation obvious, but it may not be so clear in the work environment. Many people, especially bold leaders, do not fully appreciate the constraints their teams face—or how they, themselves, add to the burden.

If you manage other people, you have the power to make their work lives enjoyable or miserable. To maintain long-term success (or at least avoid the harms described below), you must be their active, responsible, even grateful, partner.

Harm of the Myth

Acting as if others can compensate for your weak skills without your active cooperation harms you, your team, and your organization:

- **You:** Believing the myth dis-empowers you, implying that you cannot acquire or develop certain skills.
- **Your People:** The myth harms others, whether friends or executives, when you assign them responsibility without power (authority). "Make sure I get to the meeting on time," you might say. But when your assistant says the meeting starts in five minutes and you tell her you are busy, you force her to be a nag or scapegoat. "She doesn't keep me on track, as I've asked her to do," you may later complain. Yet she cannot make you do anything. You have put her in a no-win situation.
- **Your Organization:** Believing the myth harms your organization because it wastes resources. People become resentful and consume precious time stewing or trying to overcome their frustration. Some may be let go or resign unnecessarily.

    Turnover costs an organization greatly in lost productivity as replacements must be hired, trained, and brought up to speed. Some high-powered people roll through employees regularly, not realizing they are the common denominator with all these "problem" people.

The Productivity Chain Solution: Help Them Help You

You can overcome the myth that "others can make up for what I lack" by actively helping those who work with you. You can:

- **Train your team.** Begin by showing your direct-reports exactly how to help you. Taking the time to fully train your team may seem costly, but it is worth it. When you do, you strengthen your Delegation link.

- **Give prompt, direct feedback.** Providing constructive feedback is one of the most important ways you can help others help you. You can't expect people to jump "right" if you don't say how high—or to stop stepping on your toes, if you don't ask them to step off.

    Here you may want to protest, "But Communication/Relationships is my weak link in the Productivity Chain!" That may well be—but you can't give up on it. Fortunately, your weak links need to get just strong enough not to cripple you or your team.

- **Be available.** Many of my clients complain of slow or indecisive staff. Interviews and observation often reveal, however, that the staff members are "slow" because they cannot get relevant information or decisions from their supervisors.

    Regular meetings and quick responses to questions can improve your staff's output and morale. Setting aside time for those meetings may require you to strengthen your Planning link.

When you stop thinking your staff can make up for what you lack and start actively helping them help you, your productivity increases because your relationships improve. They **can** compensate for your weaknesses with your cooperation, and that makes all the difference.

29: OTHERS CAN MAKE UP FOR WHAT I LACK MYTH

Myth:	**Others can make up for what I lack.**
Reality:	I have to help them help me.
Harm Caused by Myth:	I make unreasonable demands upon my team, damaging relationships.
PC Solution:	Patience, feedback, and willingness to help them help me.
Link(s) to Strengthen:	Communication/Relationships, Delegation, Planning

Myth 30 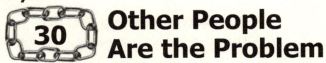 Other People Are the Problem

"My assistant is not great. She can't do as much as I wish she could, but I'm stuck with her."
—Charles, chief training officer

Charles' assistant truly does not perform well. He does not outright blame her for keeping him from accomplishing more each day. He knows he is responsible for his own life. He just wishes she would change....

That wish is Charles' real problem—not his assistant. When a coworker's frequent absences force us to do their work or we must constantly apologize for and correct the errors made by our service department, we naturally feel annoyed. But expecting "change" from the very people who frustrate us does no good—and not just because that change probably won't happen.

Wanting others to change indicates a belief in the myth that they are the problem. They must be, if their improvement is your solution. If that's the case, all you can do is wish, hope, and complain—to them and others since you can't make them change. Like Charles, you may know better than to blame them outright, but this passive "resignation" amounts to the same thing.

The myth that other people are the problem is a sister of the myth that a great staff can make up for what a supervisor lacks. In this case, however, the issue is more global.

> *If you blame others for your failures, do you credit them with your success?*
> —Unknown

Before you assume that this myth does not apply to you, remember Charles' assistant. Is there someone in your world you complain about but take no action with? Behaving as if the myth were true, even if you think you don't believe it, still keeps you stuck.

30: OTHER PEOPLE ARE THE PROBLEM MYTH

The Scapegoats

With the "others are the problem" myth, the "guilty" parties fall into several common categories, including:

- Supervisors/CEOs, for being tyrannical, untrustworthy, or passive;
- Assistants/Staff/Helpers, for being ineffective or unreliable;
- Coworkers/Peers, for being incompetent or aggressive (overstepping their bounds and/or trying to offload work);
- Clients, for being unreasonable, unresponsive, or unnecessarily time-consuming;
- Spouses/Partners, for being unsupportive, undermining, controlling, or draining;
- "Them," meaning any institution or entity that allegedly thwarts productivity, such as the government, the company, the system, and so on.

Do you recognize any of your own mental scapegoats in this list? Do any of them seem to keep you from your goals?

The Harm in Blame

Blaming is human—but it hurts you in two important ways.

- **You give away your power.** You hand the reins of your thoughts and emotions to those whose behavior annoys you. Like a horse led by the bit in its mouth, you move where the people you blame lead. They do that thing you dislike and you react—instead of acting in your own best interests.

    You may find yourself at the mercy of their moods, walking on eggshells, avoiding them, or trying to keep them happy. Your behavior starts to revolve around ***their*** needs and interests—rather than yours or the organization's.

- **You can't fix your problem if it's another person.** You lose the ability to take practical action to resolve the situation because you cannot change another person. You may inspire, support, and encourage someone to change. You may show her the way.

> When you blame others, you cannot change the situation because you cannot change them.

But unless that person wants to change, nothing will happen. If other people are the cause of your productivity problems and you cannot change other people, you are doomed.

In the end, you have two problems—your productivity shortcomings, which inspired the blame, and your negative attitude about the people involved. Your Drive link—encompassing your attitude, motivation, and effort—weakens significantly when corrosive resentment leaks onto it regularly, making your problems even more difficult to resolve.

You have, in a sense, become a victim at work. It may seem like a strong word, but it simply means someone impaired by a situation or condition.[9] Many people dislike the word, so seeing themselves from this perspective inspires them to change quickly.

The harms you experience can be big or small. One CEO complained about all the "Thank you" and "Will do!" emails that clogged his in-box. When asked if he had ever tried to discourage those kinds of messages, he replied "No." No wonder they kept occurring.

> If you are not part of the solution, you are part of the problem.

And he continued to feel harmed by them. Such small "victimizations" add up. And who is at "fault?" The email senders or the guy who won't ask them to stop? To learn more about overcoming a victim stance, see "Work's 'Victim' No More" in Chapter 1: *A New Productivity Model.*

The Productivity Chain Solution: Change Yourself

Other people may indeed initially contribute to your productivity shortfalls. There is no denying that fact. But only you can **keep** yourself in the red. You play as much a role in the situation as the other people, if not more. The faster you own it, the faster you can leave the problem behind—and regain your personal power.

You overcome the "others are to blame" myth by focusing on the reality that *you* are the only one you can change. You can use the "Don't Blame, Change" approach to do it.

30: OTHER PEOPLE ARE THE PROBLEM MYTH

> **Exercise: Don't Blame, Change**
>
> If you find yourself blaming someone for your productivity problem, try this approach. It works every time.
>
> 1. Reclaim your power to choose your response. "Own" what you choose.
> 2. Focus on you own weak links. Ask yourself how you have contributed to the problem.
> 3. Change your behavior. Strengthen your weak link(s).

1. Reclaim your power to choose.

However obnoxious, ineffective, or confusing someone else's behavior may be, you have choices. You can allow, adapt to, alter, or abandon the situation. That is your part—your responsibility—in the situation.

When you do not take responsibility for addressing a problem that affects you, you contribute to it. The old saying is true: If you are not part of the solution, you are part of the problem.

2. Focus on your own weak links.

Instead of fuming about *their* behavior, use the Productivity Chain to objectively assess and address *your* own limitations. When you focus on your own weak links, which fall within your control, your sense of integrity and self-respect blossom, along with your productivity. The Chain transmits your personal power, after all.

You can start to access that power by evaluating how you have handled this troubling situation so far. Your answers will point to links that may be weak. Here are a couple of examples of putting the focus on yourself and your own weak links.

Example 1: Assistant

There is no doubt that an incompetent assistant drains your time, tests your patience, and makes you want to "just do it yourself." However poor his performance, however, your assistant cannot damage your productivity for long without your "permission."

THE PRODUCTIVITY CHAIN

If you have an incompetent assistant, ask yourself:
- Have I clearly established his roles and responsibilities?
- Have I held him accountable for his actions or inaction through direct feedback and consequences?
- Have I clarified what he needs to do—and in what time frame—to avoid probation?
- Have I followed through when he failed to meet those criteria?
- Have I documented the issues and approached his actual supervisor (if I am not that person)?
- Do I take responsibility for my decision to keep this person working for me by focusing on the good, keeping a sense of humor about the bad, and doing all I can to protect my work from his poor behavior?

If you answered "no" to these questions, then the problem is now *you*, not your assistant. Your weak Boundary-setting, Communication/Relationships, Delegation, and Drive links have prolonged the harm done to your productivity by his behavior.

Example 2: Supervisor

Toxic or incompetent leaders harm the productivity of entire organizations. Your boss may require you to spend hours or months on projects that she discards for no good reason. She may verbally assault you in meetings. The list could go on. But if you focus only on her flaws, you will never see your own.

If you have a difficult supervisor, ask yourself:
- Have I asked my supervisor to help me prioritize projects and responsibilities when she gives me more than my share or than seems reasonable?
- Do I set boundaries when she becomes verbally abusive?
- Have I taken her aside in quiet moments to discuss how I would like to be treated?
- Have I done my best so I can approach her as a top producer?
- Have I weighed the costs and benefits of staying in this position?

30: OTHER PEOPLE ARE THE PROBLEM MYTH

- Do I take responsibility for my decision to stay by focusing on the good, keeping a sense of humor about the bad, and doing all I can to protect my team from her poor behavior?

If you answered "no" to these questions, then the problem is now you, not your supervisor. Your own weak Boundary-setting, Communication/Relationships, and Drive links have perpetuated this situation.

Does this analysis sting? It may. But it's the sting of your own power zapping back to you. When you take responsibility for your part in your relationship with an "offender," you take your reins out of his hands and firmly into your own. You regain control of your direction.

> When you take responsibility, you regain control of your direction.

(If you answered "yes" to either set of questions, particularly the last one in each list, you wouldn't still blame the other person.)

3. Change your behavior.

The final step in the process is changing your own behavior. Each relationship is a dance between two people. When one alters the steps, the other must adapt. After some stumbles, a new pattern emerges. The relationship, now re-set, may later revert, improve, or end. Your perspective on it, however, will be forever improved when you focus on changing your own attitude and actions.

To change your dance with the person you previously blamed, take positive action. Speak up, say "no," or take responsibility for doing neither. When you do, you regain your personal power and sense of control over the situation—whatever the final outcome. The change doesn't have to be large. A small shift is enough to alter the trajectory of your relationship with the other person. It strengthens your Reinvention link, too.

The "Don't Blame, Change" process helps dissolve the "other people are the problem" myth. It works, whether the situation is a minor annoyance or a soul-crushing ordeal. In some cases, like Jo's, on the next page, a sudden insight can be enough to dispel the myth.

THE PRODUCTIVITY CHAIN

Jo's Story

Jo, a product manager for an international medical device firm, felt annoyed by incessant questions from staff. "I have very little patience for people who ask questions when they can find the answers themselves," she says.

"Instead, they ask me and, as the manager, I feel I need to answer. If I don't know the answer, I look it up. They have the same tools that I do! It's just frustrating to me. Why should I waste my time if you're not going to do it yourself?" Why indeed?—especially when it keeps her from more important tasks.

"One employee said, 'I never want to call you and ask you a question that I could have easily found myself.' That's when it occurred to me that my thinking had been off," Jo continues. "I just took for granted that everybody thought the way she and I did. But everybody doesn't. Sometimes you have to train people to think a certain way."

Jo realized that she had to change. Instead of giving the answers, she needed to train her people to find the answers themselves, which she did. This strategy spared her time and aggravation. It also enabled her to take back her power and stop feeling pestered. The results: personal power and responsibility restored, productivity problem solved.

Myth:	Other people are the problem.
Reality:	I am the only one I can change.
Harm Caused by Myth:	I give away my power to change the situation by blaming others.
PC Solution:	Take responsibility for my part, focus on myself, and strengthen my own weak links.
Link(s) to Strengthen:	Drive and other links as needed

Myth 31

My Productivity Problem Has No Upside

"There's no reason for me to keep doing what I'm doing if it's not working. I'm 100 percent willing to change."
—Daniel, vice president, training and development

Once you know the behaviors and qualities that get in the way of greater productivity, you may think, as Daniel did, that you're ready to dump them. You may believe that you don't benefit from those very behaviors and qualities. Strange as it seems, though, they may serve some purpose in your life. Your productivity problem may have an upside.

Unproductive habits and beliefs are not good or bad; they just are. They usually develop to meet some needs. If you don't respect those needs, they may harden into a resistance that blindsides you, blocking your attempts to practice new, more productive habits. This internal resistance is one reason change can be so difficult.

That Behavior Has Worked for You

No behavior lasts long unless it provides some benefit—either real or imagined. When the behavior seems ineffective or even self-destructive, psychologists call these benefits "secondary gains." They have studied them in a variety of settings since Freud first defined the term.[10]

Someone with a serious illness, for example, might get extra attention from others—a secondary gain. She may "enjoy" this benefit while utterly and genuinely hating the disease itself.

You can get secondary gains—think "secret benefits"—from all sorts of seemingly negative behaviors, including over-committing, communicating poorly, procrastinating, and so on. As much as you dislike their consequences, each behavior may actually serve a valuable function.

Understanding that function reveals the gap that will be left when you change that behavior. The more successfully you fill such gaps, the more likely your new, more effective habits will last. While not all productivity problems generate secondary gains, the long-lasting ones often do.

A Smoking Example

This idea of secondary gains may sound counter-intuitive, especially when applied to work habits. What possible upside could there be from not planning your day, for example? Or feeling overwhelmed all the time?

To understand, think about smoking. Smokers know smoking poses a serious health risk. In the U.S., society generally condemns it. There are legal and physical barriers to smoking in public, for example. In the workplace, people think smokers unfairly take more or longer breaks. The smokers themselves dislike all the time their habit consumes. Standing outside in the cold and rain takes its toll. And the price of cigarettes keeps skyrocketing.

Understandably, many smokers want to quit. Yet one in five adults in the U.S. still smokes.[11] Why? Like all addictions, smoking offers plenty of secondary gains—either real or perceived. Aside from satisfying a physical craving, smoking:

- calms the nerves;
- can help prevent weight gain;
- gives the smoker something to do with his hands and mouth;
- provides an excuse to take breaks from work ("time to think," as one smoker says);
- creates a sense of collegiality with fellow smokers;
- helps the smoker "rebel" against "authority;"
- becomes so ingrained it forms a part of identity ("I'm a smoker");
- keeps the smoker from turning into the depressed, surly person she becomes when she tries to quit.

31: MY PRODUCTIVITY PROBLEM HAS NO UPSIDE MYTH

If you stop smoking, you lose these benefits. To stay stopped, you have to meet these needs in other ways. You might meditate or do yoga, for example, to calm your nerves. You may still take breaks, but stretch or chat with a friend instead of smoke. You may start an exercise program that requires you to breathe as deeply as you did when inhaling. You might begin to see yourself as a "former smoker," a new self-image.

Ex-smokers may not be fully conscious of these substitutions. They may see them only in retrospect, if at all. But they must replace their secondary gains somehow if they are to remain cigarette-free.

Potential Benefits of Weak Links

Now consider the secondary gains of your productivity problems. Although you may resist the idea at first, you might find an advantage or two. Andrew, a small business owner, realized that "having" to work weekends helped him avoid doing the household chores he disliked. His wife did them for him because he was so "swamped." As he became more productive and worked fewer hours, he needed to find a new excuse for avoiding laundry and dishwashing.

Often, unproductive habits provide belief validation. If you think "I cannot do [X]" (an attitude that weakens your Drive link), then your procrastination paralysis confirms that belief. It may not make you happy, but it satisfies the part of you that wants external reality to line up with internal reality. When your actions differ from your beliefs about yourself, you experience cognitive dissonance—an uncomfortable conflict in your mind that you must resolve in order to maintain your view of yourself and the world.[12]

The Productivity Chain Solution:
Know Your "Secret Benefits"

Awareness of your "secret benefits" gives you the power to change and grow more effectively, strengthening your Reinvention link. You can use that self-knowledge to meet the hidden needs those benefits used to satisfy. You may feel less tempted to return to old behaviors or, when tempted, better able to resist, because you

THE PRODUCTIVITY CHAIN

> **Exercise: Meet Your Needs**
>
> When you identify the needs your weak link satisfies—your secondary gains—you can find more productive ways to meet those needs.
>
> 1. Jot down your productivity problem and the weak link it represents.
> 2. Brainstorm one or two secondary gains you may get from it.
> 3. Generate one or two ways you could get a similar or better benefit while remaining highly productive.
> 4. Take that action(s) and notice what happens.

expected those temptations. No one can change habits perfectly, but knowing your "secret benefits" can minimize the depth and duration of any slip into old ways.

The "Meet Your Needs" exercise (see box) helps you clarify your secondary gain(s) and meet the underlying need(s) they represent, as Jan did. It deepens your self-awareness.

Jan's Story

Jan was a trial attorney at the height of her career. She called me because she believed she couldn't stay on top if she kept doing what she was doing. Together, we walked through the "Meet Your Needs" exercise.

1. **Her problem and weak link:** Jan's productivity problem was simple: She felt stressed and exhausted—or on the brink of it—often. She constantly worried that she was missing something. And she hated having to cover for it when she ***did*** miss something, which happened more often than she liked. So far, her errors had been minor and she wanted to keep it that way. Jan knew from her Productivity Chain Self-Assessment that her Task/Project Management link was feeble.

2. **Secondary gains:** Jan admitted that she loved the adrenaline rush of running around, getting things done at the last minute. She enjoyed the "freedom" of just showing up and flying by the seat of her pants each day, rather than monitoring her to-do's. (She also hated it at the same time.)

31: MY PRODUCTIVITY PROBLEM HAS NO UPSIDE MYTH

3. **Other ways to meet the need:** Jan said she could get that "rush" by sky diving or doing a great job, maybe even from being in control of her tasks and ahead of schedule.

4. **New approach:** Jan began to handle her work differently, using lists and reminders in new ways. She said she felt on top of everything. She worried less and felt in control. She even completed some projects in advance. It was exciting.

As the weeks went by, it became less exciting. And then almost downright boring. Gradually, Jan began reviewing her lists less often and leaving things off them. She knew she was setting herself up for a slip into her old "last minute" behavior.

Because she expected it, though, Jan recognized what was happening: she needed excitement. She decided not to sky dive but instead actively focus on the thrill of staying ahead of the curve. It had become commonplace, so she now consciously brought it to mind each day—just as she had once reminded herself of how out-of-control she was.

She also found another adrenaline source—trials. Because she was better prepared (and rested) these days, Jan enjoyed her trial work much more than she used to. "When I'm in court," she says, "my pituitary gland starts spitting out all these wonderful endorphins. I've never done heroin, but I think I've been there in the courtroom." With her excitement needs met, Jan found it easier to stay on top of her to-do's. She no longer needed the "upside" of a weak Task/Project Management link.

Myth:	**My productivity problem has no upside.**
Reality:	My current situation provides hidden benefits that meet certain needs.
Harm Caused by Myth:	I put my progress at risk if I don't address my hidden needs.
PC Solution:	Practice self-awareness and plan for temptations.
Link(s) to Strengthen:	Reinvention

Myth 32 The Problem Will Get Better by Itself

"Things are crazy right now, but they'll settle down eventually."
—Malena, Certified Public Accountant

Malena really wanted to believe the chaos in her office, schedule, and mind would naturally go away. It had in the past. She would feel overwhelmed during the busy tax season, but regain her footing during the summer lull. In recent years, however, her business had grown and the lull hadn't happened. Instead of facing the new reality, though, Malena believed the myth that her problem would get better by itself. It didn't.

Temporary Situation or Business as Usual?

Malena's hope was reasonable at first. Life and work **do** have rhythms, or at least ups and downs. Work is more hectic before and after a trip or when coworkers are absent, for example. It may be predictably busier at certain times of the year, depending on your industry. And when conflicts arise, a little patient waiting often proves useful. Some problems really do seem to resolve themselves.

Others do not. If you tend to lurch from crisis to crisis and don't make fundamental changes, that pattern will continue. If your "quiet" times are just a few notches below fever pitch, that problem will not go away by itself.

When there is so little room for error, your ability to perform can be thrown off by the slightest deviation. One sick child keeps you home from work, and suddenly you have to scramble just to stay afloat. Wishing these deep-seated, chronic problems away will not make them disappear.

32: THE PROBLEM WILL GET BETTER BY ITSELF MYTH

The Harm in the Myth

"The problem will get better by itself" myth harms your productivity in two ways. First, this passive, denial-based approach dis-empowers you. In a way, this myth is a variation on the "other people are the problem" myth. Waiting for persistent troubles to dissolve suggests that life just "happens" and all you can do is react or wish trouble away. Life does happen, but you have the power to change yourself, and therefore shape events.

This myth also causes you to spend more time in the problem than necessary. You wait and wait for the situation to improve, distracted by the sheer volume of your work. Before you know it, years have passed. *Years*. I see this happen with my clients—and others—all the time.

The Productivity Chain Solution: Compare Your Golden Age with Today

You can overcome the "it will get better by itself" myth by doing the "Compare Your Golden Age with Today" exercise. This simple—though not always easy—process helps you approach your need to change directly, thereby strengthening your Reinvention link.

Before you start, ask yourself one question: Is my productivity problem an unusual, short-term situation, or has it been the status quo for a while? If you answer "status quo," it will not change on its own. *You* have to change if you want a different outcome.

1. Analyze your Golden Age of Productivity.

Think about a time when you regularly functioned at a very high level. Your work was challenging and abundant *and* you stayed on top of it. You were "in the zone" frequently. You experienced the Power Chain (Chapter 6).

If you cannot identify such a Golden Age, focus instead on the golden moments or hours that you experience from time to time. Now write out your answers to these questions:

a. How long did your Golden Age last? Years? Days? Hours? What began it? What ended it?

b. What was the nature of your work at that time? Was it school,

THE PRODUCTIVITY CHAIN

> **Exercise: Compare Your Golden Age with Today**
>
> Once you admit you need to change, identify a time when you regularly functioned at a very high level—a Golden Age of Productivity. The factors that made you productive in the past give you insight into what might work today.
>
> 1. Analyze your Golden Age. What made it so productive?
>   a. How long did it last? What began it? What ended it?
>   b. What was the nature of your work at that time? Was it school, volunteer, paid? What field was it in? What activities did you do?
>   c. What made your high productivity possible? Was it the type of work? The environment? Some condition inside yourself?
> 2. Compare your Productivity Chain then and now. Go link by link to identify what has changed.
> 3. Strengthen your weakened or changed links.

volunteer, paid? What field was it in? What activities did you do?

c. What made your high productivity possible? Was it the type of work? The environment? Some condition inside yourself?

Identifying the factors that made you productive in the past gives you insight into what might work today.

2. Compare your Productivity Chain then and now.

Consistently high productivity depends on all twelve links in the Productivity Chain. Compare each link then and now, asking what has changed since then.

You might begin with your Health link. Have you aged much since your Golden Age? If so, your short-term memory might be less reliable than before or you might have chronic pain or illness now. You might compare your Resources link next. It might have been stronger when you knew the technology used in your office, for example, but your skills went out of date once the company switched to a new system. And so on.

32: THE PROBLEM WILL GET BETTER BY ITSELF MYTH

3. Strengthen your weakened or changed links.

Practice new, more effective habits in those areas. Obtain the resources you need. This targeted approach will help you create a new Golden Age of Productivity. If your Drive link has become impaired, for example, you would take steps to regain your motivation or productive attitude.

This process for letting go of the "it will get better by itself" myth is another way of applying the 3A's (Chapter 20: *Overcome Your Productivity Myths*). Admitting you have a new status quo and analyzing your past and present involve awareness and acceptance, the antidotes to the denial that could keep you from seeing your weak links.

As a result, practical actions you can take to strengthen your weak links begin to occur to you—the last step of the exercise. Strengthening your weakest link even a little has a positive effect on your entire Chain, increasing your overall productivity—the reward of letting go of any productivity myth.

Valarie's Story

Valarie, a university professor, found that her weakened Health link made it impossible for her to work as she once had. Her highly organized paper filing system had contributed to her productivity in the past. Quick access to information for her research projects shaved hours, even weeks, off her time.

When an illness forced her to use a cane, however, Valarie physically could not maintain her complex system. She was slower and could not reach all her cabinets anymore.

At first, she blamed herself for not performing as she once had. Accepting her limitation took time. It was tangled up in the grief over becoming disabled at age forty-three. Eventually, Valarie realized she would not regain her former productivity level unless she took action.

Her Golden Age of Productivity analysis showed her that she needed to invest in a more effective information management system, and get help to run it. Her physical limitations meant that system couldn't require much movement. A digital filing and indexing software, operated by a student intern, fit the bill.

THE PRODUCTIVITY CHAIN

With support from her beefed-up Resources and Delegation links, Valarie's Health link no longer damaged her Organization of Objects/Data link, and her research projects began to move forward again.

Bottom Line

Comparing your Golden Age of Productivity and your current situation in light of the Productivity Chain gives you valuable insight into ways to improve your performance today. It tells you which links to strengthen. It can also help you view your situation more objectively and be less critical of yourself, as Valarie found. Best of all, it enables you to stop believing the myth that your problem will somehow get better by itself.

> *If you want something to change, then **you** need to change something.*
> Carol, vice president

"I know my way isn't working when a quarter, then a year, then two or three years go by, and nothing's changed," says Carol, the corporate vice president whose story opened this book.

"If I keep doing the same things, the same way, and I expect different results, then I might as well just check into a mental hospital, because it's insane. If you want something to change, then ***you*** need to change something."

Myth:	**The situation will get better by itself.**
Reality:	I have to change myself if I want a different outcome.
Harm Caused by Myth:	I spend more time in the problem by denying it and I undermine my own power to create a solution.
PC Solution:	Honest self-appraisal.
Link(s) to Strengthen:	Reinvention and any affected link in the Chain

CASE STUDY: KAREN

Karen's Story

Karen's experience illustrates the interaction among the links in the Productivity Chain. When her Health and Boundary-setting links were damaged, no amount of strength in her other links could fully compensate. When she focused on strengthening those links, her overall productivity and enjoyment of life improved.

SUMMARY

The Professional: Karen is CEO of a promotional products supply company

Strong Links: Decision-making, Goal-setting/Prioritization, Task/Project Management

Solutions that Worked—Strengthening the Weak Links:

- Boundary-setting: Set limits and hold staff accountable for sub-standard performance.
- Delegation: Provide adequate oversight of staff.
- Health: Address physical health issues diligently.

Karen's promotional products supply company employs about twenty people. She founded it fifteen years ago and always turned a profit. Her clear goals, strong decision-making skills, and ability to manage her tasks and projects effectively made her highly productive. Customers often called with last-minute orders and Karen built her reputation on her fast response.

Still, she had the sense that the business often operated in crisis mode. Sometimes that weakness showed. "We've been late on proposals," she admits. "For one in particular, a federal project, the proposal was due at noon. I hit 'Send' at noon exactly, though I should have hit 'Send' at noon the day before. They received it at 12:01:45 and refused to look at it because it was late. I don't know if we would have won it, but we didn't get the opportunity."

Usually such occurrences were rare. Then Karen began having trouble with her health. Her productivity fell sharply because she felt terrible and took time off. "I've had two

THE PRODUCTIVITY CHAIN

surgeries in the past four years. I would be on a roll, and then I'd get sick," she notes. "And then I'd have to get back up and do it all over again."

When she needed support the most, her staff did not provide it. Karen had long complained about the poor work habits of some key people, but she never held them accountable for their performance. She just powered through herself. "I'd find so many things undone and I'd try to do them myself, instead of saying 'I have to let you go,'" she says.

Powering through was no longer an option. "I had to lower my expectations of myself. It was really frustrating because I couldn't get done the stuff that I could do normally." Even her Attention Deficit Disorder (ADD), her sometimes productivity ally, stopped helping her.

"The one advantage of ADD is that you have the ability to hyper-focus, and you can get stuff done in a shorter period of time than anybody else can, and people kind of get blown away," she explains. "But you're not like that all the time." With her illness, Karen was like that less and less.

With her Productivity Chain in mind, Karen made targeted changes, starting with her Health link. She made her physical well-being her top priority, taking the time she needed for medical appointments, rest, recuperation, and stress-reduction.

> Karen made her physical well-being her top priority.

"I very aggressively pursued recovery," she says. "Had a really good doctor on my side and took care of myself." She began taking walks and gardening again as her health improved, practices she had given up when she was so ill.

As she regained her energy, Karen focused on her weak Boundary-setting link, which had disabled her Delegation link. She began clarifying roles and expectations, especially with her Comptroller, Sandra. Sandra was a highly-skilled, moody, procrastinating perfectionist. She turned the smallest assignments into the biggest projects, and let her drama-filled personal life interfere during the work day.

On the other hand, she also found ways to save the company money and she was honest. The previous Comptroller had

CASE STUDY: KAREN

embezzled a great deal of money, leaving the business in debt. Karen had been so grateful to hire someone she trusted that she had not set firm limits with Sandra. She complained and encouraged, but never laid down the law or gave consequences.

This time, Karen tightened the reins. She gave deadlines, followed up promptly, and did not accept excuses. "I've been saying 'no' to Sandra a lot more, putting my foot down," she notes. "It gets easier when I practice it."

She even set limits on conversations, which Sandra used as a way to avoid working. "She might ask me how my daughter was doing," says Karen. "I'd answer 'Oh, she's fine,' and she'd start in about her daughter. I'd feel obligated to listen to her because she listened to me. Mine was twenty seconds and hers was twenty minutes."

That behavior came to a halt. "I've tried to drop any emotion out of it and not let my guard down and talk about personal junk. I'm separating the task from the emotional kind of thing," Karen explains.

> Karen tightened the reins. She gave deadlines, followed up, and did not accept excuses.

After several months under the new regime, Sandra quit. Once the expectations were clear, the deadlines enforced, and the oversight present, she no longer wanted to work in that environment. It had been Karen's greatest fear for so long. When it happened, it was a relief.

Almost immediately, she replaced Sandra with someone who had an equally strong skill set and none of the baggage. And she has used her strengthened delegation skills to set a more powerful tone with her new Comptroller from the start.

With her health restored and support in place, Karen's business picked up again. Through her productivity journey, she has discovered what makes it all worthwhile. "At the end of the day, I come home to a house where I'm loved with people I love," she says.

"Nothing is perfect," she continues. "But my destiny is in my hands. If I fall, I just brush myself off and get up and get going. And I take time off now. I do it without guilt anymore. I take more breaks, and I find I'm more productive as a result." Karen was reaping the rewards of a stronger Productivity Chain.

# Afterword

I hope the Productivity Chain enables you to view your work in a new, more empowering light. I hope it helps you identify and pursue precise, actionable solutions for your productivity problems, saving you from vague or misdirected efforts.

Finally, I hope it puts to rest the harmful myths about productivity that interfere with your becoming more effective in your work and your life.

Please let me know what you think of *The Productivity Chain*, and how you have strengthened your own Chain. You can reach me at *www.CaseyMooreInc.com*.

Best wishes,

Casey Moore

Appendix

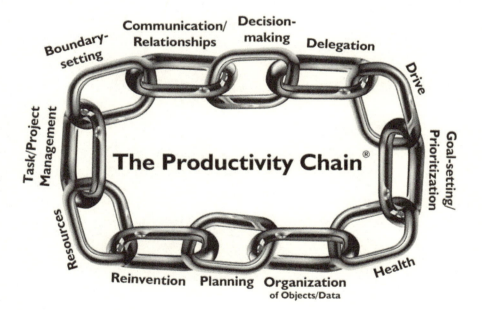

Appendix A

Productivity Chain Self-Assessment

Before you begin your journey to enhance your workplace performance, identify your starting position. Clarifying your productivity strengths and weaknesses reveals which areas to target for improvement.

To get a detailed and accurate evaluation, take the full Productivity Chain Self-Assessment at *www.CaseyMooreInc.com*. After completing this online assessment, you get an instant report detailing your productivity strengths and weaknesses. It also offers specific suggestions to improve your effectiveness.

You can take a short productivity quiz on the site, too. Your instant email report identifies which links might warrant further evaluation. It also provides a general tip for improving each link.

Appendix B

Instant Reframe Examples

The chart below illustrates examples of the Productivity Chain Instant Reframe described in Chapter 4: *Identify Solutions*. Reframing a problem generates new solutions. It puts the focus on you—the only one you can change. The problems below appear in order of their weak link in the Productivity Chain (PC), as indicated in the third column.

Symptom	Conventional Problem Definition & Solution	PC Problem Definition & Solution
You feel taken advantage of by others.	*Problem:* You think you are too nice. *Solution:* You hope they change because you certainly don't want to be mean to them.	*Problem:* You have difficulty setting limits and standing up for yourself. (**Boundary-setting link** is weak.) *Solution:* Get assertiveness training, work with a coach, set boundaries, and so on.
Your direct-reports make mistakes frequently, which they then try to hide.	*Problem:* They are timid and need to learn to take responsibility. *Solution:* Tell them to own up to mistakes immediately; you won't punish them for errors.	*Problem:* You have a history of blowing up in anger and have created an unsafe environment. (**Communication/Relationships link** is weak.) *Solution:* Improve your self-management and mend relationships by proving over time that you can be trusted with news of mistakes.
You feel overwhelmed by all the information coming at you each day.	*Problem:* You get too many emails. *Solution:* Spend more time on emails.	*Problem:* You don't make decisions about the emails, so they accumulate and cause stress. (**Decision-making link** is weak.) *Solution:* Practice ruthless decision-making, taking action on each email before moving to the next.

APPENDIX B: INSTANT REFRAME EXAMPLES

Symptom	Conventional Problem Definition & Solution	PC Problem Definition & Solution
Your assistant sometimes doesn't do what you assign.	*Problem:* She avoids what she doesn't like to do but it's difficult to find good help. You're stuck. *Solution:* Remind her about it again and hope she improves.	*Problem:* You avoid holding her accountable in a direct way. (**Delegation link** is weak.) *Solution:* Get the training or support you need to have those uncomfortable conversations and come up with an action plan for her to follow.
You are losing interest in work and are just going through the motions.	*Problem:* The work isn't challenging anymore and the environment is not stimulating enough. *Solution:* Find a new position.	*Problem:* You have settled into a routine and lost motivation. (**Drive link** is weak.) *Solution:* Identify ways to improve your own performance or take on a new, challenging, growth-inducing responsibility.
You are not hitting your performance numbers.	*Problem:* The company takes up your time with administrative reports and meetings. *Solution:* Work longer hours to hit goals.	*Problem:* You are not prioritizing your tasks to put your goals first and "admin" second. (**Goal-setting/Prioritization link** is weak.) *Solution:* Get an accountability partner to hold you to spending sixty percent of your time on goal activities.
Your life feels out of balance—too much time at work, not enough time for personal matters.	*Problem:* You have too much to do. *Solution:* You need to work harder.	*Problem:* You don't protect your personal time, so evenings and weekends fail to refresh you. (**Health link** is weak.) *Solution:* Schedule relaxation time with no cell phone or email access.
Your office is cluttered and you often can't find the papers or electronic documents you need as fast as you would like.	*Problem:* You are not organized enough and have too much stuff. *Solution:* Periodically neaten things up, curse it when it falls apart, and do the best you can.	*Problem:* You have not identified homes for items nor systems to maintain them. (**Organization of Objects/Data link** is weak.) *Solution:* Take time to plan simple systems you can maintain readily.

THE PRODUCTIVITY CHAIN

Symptom	Conventional Problem Definition & Solution	PC Problem Definition & Solution
You never seem to have time for the important projects that have no set deadlines.	*Problem:* You are too busy. *Solution:* Work late or let them go; you can't do it all.	*Problem:* You don't allocate time for high-priority activities. **(Planning link** is weak.) *Solution:* Make appointments with a project and have an accountability partner help you stick to it.
You resent recent corporate decisions. It just seems like change for change's sake.	*Problem:* The company's new initiative is throwing a wrench into operations. *Solution:* Just wait it out; it will probably fail soon anyway.	*Problem:* You are resisting change—change that is inevitable. **(Reinvention link** is weak.) *Solution:* Identify the positive in the situation and try to make the transition as smooth as possible.
Reports take a long time to produce and you often feel like you're reinventing the wheel.	*Problem:* The company requires too many reports. *Solution:* Work late if necessary.	*Problem:* You are not using the company's custom software to its full potential. **(Resources link** is weak.) *Solution:* Get more training and take time to learn how to maximize the software's power.
Some tasks are slipping through the cracks and it is causing problems.	*Problem:* You are not organized enough. *Solution:* Get more organized—maybe buy a new planner or software.	*Problem:* You have too many task-management "systems," including stacks, sticky notes, and scrawled to-do lists. **(Task/Project Management link** is weak.) *Solution:* Create one funnel to manage all activities.

Appendix

Productivity-Related Terms

All productivity-related factors—both liabilities and assets—have a place in the Productivity Chain. Most fall within a specific link; a few span more than one. See Chapter 7: *A Guiding Framework* for a graphic depiction of the factors by link.

Addiction (*Health link*)—Addictions can take many forms. You may be addicted to substances, such as alcohol, drugs, or nicotine; or to behaviors, such as gambling, overeating, or sexually acting-out. Although many experts classify addictions as diseases, others argue they are not. Everyone ***can*** agree, however, that they cause "dis-ease." They divert attention and energy, impair judgment, consume time, and damage self-esteem and relationships. They certainly decrease productivity. (See Workaholism.)

Ambition (*Drive link*)—A desire to succeed can contribute to productivity by fortifying the Drive link. Alone, however, ambition is not enough—despite conventional "wisdom" that says if you want something badly enough, you will get it.

Brain-Based Conditions (*Health link*)—Brain-based conditions are mental factors that affect productivity. They include, among others:

- *Anxiety*, which inhibits focused action;
- *Attention Deficit Disorder (ADD)*, which inhibits Organization of Objects/Data, among other links. It is officially called Attention Deficit Hyperactivity Disorder but, since hyperactivity is not required for the diagnosis, this book uses the less-confusing ADD;
- *Depression*, either Major or Bipolar, which decreases energy and motivation (Drive link) or, in the case of the "manic" aspect of bipolar, exaggerates it without restraint;

THE PRODUCTIVITY CHAIN

- *Learning Disabilities*, such as dyslexia, which interfere with learning and written communication;
- *Traumatic Brain Injury*, which may affect concentration and language ability, among other functions.

Burnout (*Drive link*)—Burnout occurs when motivation is lost and outlook sours. It involves a cluster of symptoms, such as emotional fatigue and even physical health problems. Burnout can be severe, as when professional caregivers grow calloused and insensitive to their patients. In such cases, a rupture of the Drive link has occurred.

More often, people get "crispy around the edges," finding it more and more difficult to muster energy for their work day. Their Drive link is "just" strained.

Chronic Disorganization (*Organization of Objects/Data link*)—Chronic disorganization (CD) is not a medical or psychiatric diagnosis, but it is a recognized condition that affects many. Judith Kolberg, founder of the Institute for Challenging Disorganization (formerly the National Study Group on Chronic Disorganization), states that to have CD, you must meet these three criteria:

1. "The persistence of severe disorganization over a long period of time;
2. "A daily undermining of one's quality of life by disorganization; and
3. "A history of failed self-help efforts."[1]

The definition continues to evolve, based on new research. It now includes "the expectation of future disorganization."[2] For more information, go to *www.challengingdisorganization.com*.

Context (*All links*)—The Productivity Chain, and all its links, exists in the context of location, history, societal, and cultural norms, current economic climate, and so on. These factors have an often-overlooked impact on personal productivity. A highly effective salesperson in the U.S. might have poorer results in Africa, for instance, because of cultural and resource differences, the language barrier, and so on. Similarly, a CEO might be productive until an unexpected technological advancement makes her company's product obsolete. Understanding your contexts puts your links' strengths in a broader perspective.

APPENDIX C: PRODUCTIVITY-RELATED TERMS

Creativity (*Reinvention link*)—Creativity is the ability to approach problems and situations in novel ways, often by combining seemingly unrelated ideas. Since the Reinvention link includes the re-creation of yourself, systems, or plans, creativity falls within that link.

Discipline (*Drive link*)—Discipline is the ability to maintain self-control and orderly behavior.[3] It helps determine your mental approach to work, which puts it in the Drive link. Discipline also enhances your ability to develop and maintain productive habits. It fortifies other links, especially Boundary-setting.

Effectiveness (*All links*)—Effectiveness means taking the actions that will (most likely) produce the results you seek. It is doing the best thing in the best way, which is why, in the Productivity Chain model, effective action requires efficiency, as well. It comes as a result of the cooperation of every link in the Chain.

Efficiency (*All links*)—Efficiency means doing a task in the most direct, least-wasteful way. It involves an economy of movement, time, and effort. Every link contributes to efficiency. It is possible, however, to efficiently take ineffective action.

Initiative (*Drive link*)—Initiative is the willingness to step forward and take action, to volunteer, to take ownership. It is a quality that separates leaders from followers. Since it is about approach, willingness, and energy, it falls under the Drive link.

Intelligence (*Resources link*)—Intelligence refers to both innate aptitude and abilities that can be developed. It includes all types of intelligence, from that measured by standard IQ tests (which are primarily verbal- and math-oriented) to Emotional Intelligence and others. (See Howard Gardner's *Frames of Mind: The Theory of Multiple Intelligences.*[4])

Interruptions (*Boundary-setting link*)—Interruptions come in many forms, both external (e.g., email, phone, drop-by's) and internal (e.g., distracting thoughts, aching back). Boundary-setting enables you to prevent, manage, and minimize any kind of interruptions.

Job Fitness (*Resources link*)—Job fitness is an often-overlooked factor in productivity. It is difficult to perform well in a job that does not suit you. If you hate public speaking, for example, it may be difficult to be an effective corporate trainer. There are degrees of

THE PRODUCTIVITY CHAIN

fitness, of course. It is part of the Resources link because self-knowledge enables you to find work that fits.

Leadership (*All links*)—Leadership, which includes inspiring others to act, relates to People Management (see below), although it goes well beyond it. It is a link-leaper.

Mindfulness (*All links*)—It means paying attention purposefully and non-judgmentally in the present moment. Practicing it has a powerful positive effect on every link in the Productivity Chain.

Order (*Organization of Objects/Data link*)—Keeping things and information in order (as opposed to chaos) is a function of the Organization of Objects/Data link. Order facilitates productivity because it makes it easier for you (and others) to find objects and data as needed. The level of order needed for top productivity depends on the person. A very orderly environment sparks creativity in some, while a little disorder has the same effect on others.

People Management (*All links*)—Supervising one person or heading a company of thousands requires you to manage other people, not just yourself. Because people management is such a complex and human-focused endeavor, you could say that it "leaps" links, encompassing every other link in the Chain. It includes delegation, of course, but requires much more than giving assignments and providing oversight.

It involves gaining and providing organizational resources, decision-making for the group, communicating with and navigating relationships within the group and between the group and the larger organization, and so on.

Perfectionism (*Drive link*)—This productivity-killer prevents you from knowing when your work has to be perfect or close to it (e.g., doing brain surgery) and when it can be good enough (e.g., writing notes during a staff meeting). Perfectionism wastes time and leads to paralysis. It falls under the Drive link because it affects attitude and motivation.

Personality (*Resources link*)—Anyone can be productive; it is not a personality trait, but rather the combination of many factors—and subject to change. Personality traits do influence your productivity preferences, however. The Myers-Briggs Type Indicator, the most well-known model of personality types,

APPENDIX C: PRODUCTIVITY-RELATED TERMS

considers where people draw energy, for example. Introverts, who draw energy from within, may be most productive when alone while extraverts get energized and produce more when in a group.

Because the many facets of personality can affect any link, it may be considered another "link leaper." As a tool of self-knowledge, however, it falls under the Resources link.

Problem-solving (*Decision-making link*)—Problem-solving is a valuable skill, requiring high-level cognitive skills. It involves problem definition, assessment of solution options, and decision-making (the link where it resides). In a sense, the Productivity Chain is a problem-solving model.

Processing Modalities (*Resources link*)—People instinctively prefer certain modalities to perceive and process information, to learn, and to work. In her book, *Processing Modalities Guide*,[5] Denslow Brown identifies nine distinct modalities: Auditory, Cognitive, Emotional, Intuitive, Kinesthetic, Tactile, Taste/Smell, Verbal, and Visual.

Adopting work systems and habits that align with your processing modalities preferences promotes greater productivity and satisfaction. Modalities fall under the Resources link because they require self-knowledge to be useful.

Procrastination (*Drive link, usually*)—This productivity crusher can operate in different links. It resides in the Drive link when it relates to conscious task avoidance, such as caused by perfectionism or resentment. This procrastination type is the most common.

Some procrastination occurs because of a weak Task/Project Management link, rather than avoidance. You may break down a project, for instance—not avoiding it at all—but lack a way to integrate the project tasks with your other to-do's. In the rush of day-to-day business, they don't get done.

On rare occasions, procrastination may stem from an inner wisdom that compels you to delay while some idea or circumstance ripens. With a little awareness, you can make a powerful decision to "back burner" a project temporarily. Consciously prioritizing a project or task onto the back burner is not procrastination.

Resentment (*Drive link*)—Many emotions affect performance; they usually apply to the Health link. Resentment, however, can become an entrenched attitude. As such, it falls under the Drive link. Unless you release it, resentment poisons productivity. People waste countless hours at work and home ruminating on slights and planning responses. The person most harmed by resentment is the person who nurses it.

Resilience (*Reinvention link*)—Resilience refers to the ability of people to recover from, and perhaps even grow as a result of, difficulties or challenges—life changes thrust upon them.

Talent (*Resources link*)—We all have gifts and talents. Yours may be job-specific, such as a gift for seeing how to lead the market in your industry. Other talents relate to transferrable skills, such as writing or speaking. Often, someone's special talent is an average ability honed by long practice. It is a resource, and so fits that link.

Teamwork (*Communication/Relationships link*)—Whether the team is a temporary, project-focused, interdepartmental group of individuals or everyone in an organization as a whole, the "teamwork" approach is designed to promote positive relationships and facilitate clear communication, placing it within the Communication/Relationships link.

Time Management (*All links*)—In Productivity Chain terms, "time management" fits in the Planning link, with its scheduling and time allocation. It is counted as a link-leaper, however, because using time most wisely requires cooperation of all the links. For most people, "time management" is as vague a term as the conventional "getting organized;" people use it, too, to mean "productivity."

Workaholism (*Drive link, Health link*)—Workaholism is a type of addictive behavior. It is a complex phenomenon, but essentially the workaholic uses work and busy-ness to feel good or avoid feeling bad. As an addiction, it belongs in the Health link. Because it represents a very specific motive for working, however, it belongs in the Drive link as well. (See Addiction.)

Work Ethic (*Drive link*)—Your work ethic is your approach to work, regardless of the type of activity or your feelings towards it. A strong work ethic involves treating any responsibility with a strong effort, dedication, commitment to quality, punctuality, and a positive attitude. Because it includes approach, effort, and attitude, work ethic belongs in the Drive link.

Appendix D

Productivity-Related Resources

Here are some popular and excellent productivity-related books and other resources that I recommend. They are listed alphabetically under the link in the Productivity Chain they *especially* enhance. Those that address many links or specific topics appear at the end.

Boundary-setting Link

Boundaries by Henry Cloud, PhD, and John Townsend, Ph.D. (Note: this book has a Christian focus.)

The Gift of Fear by Gavin deBecker

When I Say No I Feel Guilty by Manuel Smith, Ph.D.

Communication/Relationships Link

Fierce Conversations by Susan Scott

How to Reduce Workplace Conflict and Stress by Anna Maravelas

Mastering Respectful Confrontation by Joe Weston

Nonviolent Communication by Marshall Rosenberg, Ph.D.

Decision-making Link

Harvard Business Review on Decision Making from HRB

How We Decide by Jonah Lehrer

Smart Choices by John Hammond Ralph Keeney and Howard Raiffa

Delegation Link

Don't Do Delegate! by James Jenks and John Kelly

How to Delegate by Robert Heller

Drive Link

Drive by Daniel Pink

It's About Time by Linda Sapadin, Ph.D. with Jack Maguire

The Power of Full Engagement by Jim Loehr and Tony Schwartz

Goal-setting/Prioritization Link

Creating Your Best Life by Caroline Adams Miller, MAPP, and Michael Frisch, Ph.D.

Three Big Questions by Dave Phillips

Health Link

Off Balance On Purpose by Dan Thurmon

The Power of Full Engagement by Jim Loehr and Tony Schwartz

Why Zebras Don't Get Ulcers by Robert Sapolsky, Ph.D.

Organization of Objects/Data Link

But I Might Need It Someday! by Patty Kreamer, CPO®

Institute for Challenging Disorganization,

THE PRODUCTIVITY CHAIN

ChallengingDisorganization.com

National Association of Productivity and Organizing Professionals, *NAPO.net*

Organize Your Work Day in No Time by K.J. McCorry

Organizing from the Inside Out by Julie Morgenstern

Taming the Paper Tiger in a Digital World by Barbara Hemphill at *BarbaraHemphill.com* e-book

Planning Link

Time Management from the Inside Out by Julie Morgenstern

Reinvention Link

The Inside-Out Revolution by Michael Neill

The Little Book of Big Change by Amy Johnson, Ph.D.

One Small Step Can Change Your Life by Robert Maurer, Ph.D.

The Power of Habit by Charles Duhigg

Who Moved My Cheese? by Spencer Johnson and Kenneth Blanchard

Resources Link

BarOn Emotional Quotient-Inventory (EQ-i®) re: emotional intelligence

DISC assessment re: behavior

Kolbe Index re: behavior mode

Myers-Briggs Type Indicator re: personality types

The Introvert Advantage by Marti Olsen Laney, Psy.D.

Processing Modalities Guide by Denslow Brown, MCC, CPO®, CPO-CD®

Task/Project Management Link

The Complete Idiot's Guide to Project Management by Michael Campbell, PMP

The Fundamentals of Planning by Peter Capezio 2000

Getting Things Done by David Allen

How to Get Organized without Resorting to Arson by Liz Franklin

Project Management by Andy Bruce and Ken Langdon

Total Workday Control by Patrick Lencioni

Multiple-Link Books

These books affect several or all links:

Eat That Frog! by Brian Tracy

Never Check E-Mail in the Morning by Julie Morgenstern

The 7 Habits of Highly Effective People by Stephen Covey, Ph.D.

Time Power by Brian Tracy

Your Brain at Work by David Rock

Mindfulness

Headspace app at *headspace.com*

Rewire Your Brain for Love by Marsha Lucas Ph.D.

Attention Deficit Disorder

These books target those with ADD but their ideas can help anyone:

ADD-Friendly Ways to Organize Your Life by Judith Kolberg and Kathleen Nadeau, Ph.D.

More Attention Less Deficit by Ari Tuckman, Ph.D.

Appendix E  Endnotes

Preface

1 "Mindfulness can literally change your brain." *Harvard Business Review,* by Congleton, Hölzel, and Lazar, 2011.

2 "Mindfulness practice leads to increases in regional brain gray matter density." *Psychiatry Research: Neuroimaging,* Vol. 191, No. 1, by Hölzel, et al., 2011.

3 *ibid.*

Section I: The Productivity Chain

1 *Getting Things Done* by David Allen, Penguin Books, New York, 2001, p. 37.

2 *Webster's New World Dictionary: Third College Edition,* Prentice Hall, New York, 1991.

3 *Webster's New World Dictionary.*

4 *Drive* by Daniel Pink, Riverhead Books, New York, 2009, p. 72.

5 *"Stop focusing on your strengths." Harvard Business Review IdeaCast* by Chamorro-Permuzic with Sarah Green Carmichael. Jan. 21, 2016.

6 *Webster's New World Dictionary.*

Section II: The Twelve Links

1 *Harvard Business Review on Decision Making,* Harvard Business School Press, Boston, 2001, p. 3.

2 *Eat That Frog!* by Brian Tracy, Berrett-Koehler Publishers, Inc., San Francisco, 2001, p. 22.

Permission statement: "Brian Tracy is the most listened to audio author on personal and business success in the world today. His fast-moving talks and seminars on leadership, sales, managerial effectiveness and business strategy are loaded with powerful, proven ideas and strategies that people can immediately apply to get better results in every area. For more information, please go to *www.briantracy.com.*"

3 Barbara Hemphill even trademarked "Clutter is Postponed Decisions.®"

4 "A Logical Choice" by Gary Belsky, *Real Simple* magazine, March 2004, p. 194.

5 *The Gift of Fear* by Gavin deBecker, Dell Publishing, New York, 1997.

6 *Webster's New World Dictionary: Third College Edition,* Prentice Hall, New York, 1991.

7 *Creating Your Best Life* by Caroline Adams Miller, MAPP, and Dr. Michael Frisch, Sterling, New York, 2009, p. 50.

8 *ibid,* p. 51.

9 *The 7 Habits of Highly Effective People* by Dr. Stephen Covey, Simon and Schuster, New York, 1989, p. 151.

10 *Getting Things Done* by David Allen, Penguin Books, New York, 2001, p. 49.

11 *Eat That Frog!* by Brian Tracy, Berrett-Koehler Publishers, Inc., San Francisco, 2001, p. 89.

12 *Making Work Work* (renamed *Never Check E-Mail in the Morning*) by Julie Morgenstern, Simon and Schuster, New York, 2004, p. 72.

13 *Taming the Paper Tiger at Work* by Barbara Hemphill, Kiplinger's Books, Washington, DC, 2002, p. 23.

14 Kaizen—"a change toward good"—has been credited with the success of Toyota and others (e.g., "Toyota stumbles but its 'kaizen' cult endures" by James B. Kelleher, *Reuters.com*, Feb. 8, 2010).

15 "A Brain-Based Approach to Coaching" by David Rock, based on an interview with Jeffrey M. Schwartz, M.D., *International Journal of Coaching in Organizations*, 2006, 4(2), pp. 32-43.

16 Someone described a cartoon from *The New Yorker* that depicted this scenario.

17 *Getting Things Done* by David Allen, Penguin Books, New York, 2001, p. 37.

Section III: Productivity Myths

1 "Were You Born on the Wrong Continent?: America's Misguided Culture of Overwork" by Alex Yung, *Salon.com*, August 25, 2010.

2 Workaholics Anonymous, *Workaholics-anonymous.org*.

3 National Association of Productivity and Organizing Professionals, *NAPO.net*.

4 *Webster's New World Dictionary: Third College Edition*, Prentice Hall, New York, 1991.

5 "Career Advice from Powerful ADHD Executives" by Lois Gilman, *ADDitude Magazine*, *ADDitudemag.com*, December/January 2005.

6 "Seth Godin: Profile of a Marketing Guru" by Jessie Scanlon, Bloomberg's *Businessweek.com*, September 24, 2008.

7 "Cognitive Outlaws" by Joann Ellison Rodgers, *Psychology Today*, Vol. 44, No. 1, Jan/Feb. 2011.

8 *Outliers* by Malcolm Gladwell, Little, Brown & Co., New York, 2008, p. 47.

9 *Webster's New World Dictionary*.

10 *Introductory Lectures on Psychoanalysis*, Vol. 16, by Sigmund Freud, Hogarth Press, London, 1917.

11 American Heart Association, *Heart.org*, National Health Interview Survey (NHIS), 2008, National Center for Health Statistics.

12 *Encyclopedia Brittanica*, "cognitive dissonance," *Britannica.com*.

Appendix

1 *What Every Professional Organizer Needs to Know about Chronic Disorganization* by Judith Kolberg, Squall Press, p. 4.

2 Institute for Challenging Disorganization, *ChallengingDisorganization.com*

3 *Webster's New World Dictionary: Third College Edition*, Prentice Hall, New York, 1991.

4 *Frames of Mind: The Theory of Multiple Intelligences* by Howard Gardner, Basic Books, New York, 1993.

5 *Processing Modalities Guide: Identify and Use Specific Strengths for Better Functioning...for Organizers, Coaches—and Those Who Want to Live with More Ease and Effectiveness—and Less Frustration*, by Denslow Brown, Hickory Guild Press, Drury, MO, 2010.

Index

3A's, 124, 152-153, 167, 211, *see acceptance, awareness, action*
3O's, 99
4 Pillars, 102-103

A Game, 73
acceptance, x, 87, 152-153, 173-174, 181
action, vii, 9-10, 24-25, 152-153, 181, 205
    examples of, 35-36
addiction, 204, 221
agenda, 117
Allen, David, 95
ambition, 225
assertiveness, 4, 17, 47-49, 66-67, 69, 136, 220 *see communication*
Attention Deficit Disorder, xii, 100-101, 172-173, 214, 223
attitude, defined, 83
autonomy, 23
awareness, viii, 20, 41, 64, 102, 149, 152, 153, 178-181

balance, defined, 98-99
behavior, 63, *see communication*
blame, 22, 27, 149, 196-202
Boundary-setting link, xi, 2, 3, 5, 45, 157, 167, 185, 200-201, 220
    see Productivity Chain
    story about, 13, 16, 17, 29, 42, 47, 48, 55-60, 157-158, 213-215
brain-based conditions, 98, 223
Brown, Denslow, 227, 230
burnout, 103, 167, 226
busy-ness, 115, 164-167, 178

Chain, *see Productivity Chain*
Chain Reaction, 16-17, 158
chronic disorganization, xii, 13, 45, 224
clarity, defined, 40
clutter, 106, 110, 113, 139
    mental, 28, 40, 139
cognitive dissonance, 205
communication, 61-63, *see Communication/Relationships link*
Communication/Relationships link, xi, viii, 2, 4-5, 16, 45, 61-69, 200-201, 220 *see Productivity Chain*
    story about, 13, 16, 29-30, 34-35, 47, 49, 65-66
context, 45, 62, 224, *see communication*
control, x, xiii, xvi, 1, 9, 15, 25, 38, 40, 56, 92, 106, 115, 199, 201
Covey, Dr. Stephen, 95, 230
creativity, 45, 225
crisis, 11, 19, 25, 156

data, defined, 109, *see Organization of Objects/Data link*
deBecker, Gavin, 74, 229
Decision-making link, xi, 2, 4-5, 45, 70-75, 156-159, 220
    see Productivity Chain
    story about, 30, 33, 72-73, 157-158
Delegation link, xi, 2, 4-5, 16, 45, 72, 76-81, 176, 177, 191-195, 200, 221
    see Productivity Chain
    story about, 16, 27, 29, 77-78, 80, 145-146, 213-215
delivery, 62, *see communication*
depression, 14, 98, 223
discipline, 45, 168, 225
disorganization, 108, 172-173, 189
Drive link, xi, viii, 2, 4-5, 45, 82-88, 162,

188-190, 198, 205, 221
   see Productivity Chain
   story about, 14, 16, 29-30, 32, 34-35, 49, 84-86, 162
Drucker, Peter, 71

effectiveness, defined, 45, 225
efficiency, defined, 45, 225
effort, x, xv, 2, 4, 8, 45, 83
email overload cure, 28-31
emotional health, defined, 98
emotional intelligence, *see intelligence*
energy, 3, 14, 22, 28, 40-41, 45, 48, 55, 59, 60, 65, 77, 82-83, **86**, 91, 95, 97-103, 106, 112, 125-126, 133, 135, 161, 164-165, 174, 181-182, 187
Exercises, *see Take Action*
   "A" Game, 73
   Compare Golden Age with Today, 210
   Don't Blame, Change, 199
   Meet Your Needs, 206
   Raise Your Time Awareness, 180
   Three Good Reasons, 68
   What's Your Mythology?, 150
   When Are You Organizing "Just Enough"—or "Too Much?", 109
expectations, 79

flexibility, defined, 124, *see Resources link*
Four Pillars of Balance, 102-103, *see balance*

Gardner, Howard, 227
Gladwell, Malcolm, 189
goal-setting, 90, *see Goal-setting/Prioritization link*
Goal-setting/Prioritization link, xi, 2, 4-5, 45, 72, 89-96, 167, 181, 221
   see Productivity Chain
   story about, 15, 16, 30, 42, 93, 162
Godin, Seth, 172
Golden Age of Productivity, 38, 209-212

Health link, xi, 2, 4-5, 45, 97-105, 221
   see Productivity Chain
   story about, 13, 14, 27, 30, 49, 100, 101, 157-158, 212, 213-215
Hemphill, Barbara, 113

humility, 103, 157-158

initiative, 45, 225
Instant Reframe, 25-26, 31-32, 220-222
   see Productivity Chain Analysis
Institute for Challenging Disorganization, 224
intelligence, 45, 100, 225
interactions, link, *see link interactions*
interruptions, 45, 56, 60, 225
intuition, 45, 74-75

job fitness, 45, 132, 225
job-related skills, *see skills, job-related*

kaizen, 125
kindness, 45, 59, 67-68
knowledge (of self, job), 45, 132-133
Kolberg, Judith, 224, 230

leadership, 45, 226
learning, 35-36, 45, 132-136, 188-190
link interactions, 5-6, 15-17, *see*
   Chain Reaction
   Power Chain
   Productivity Chain
links,
   how to strengthen, 33-36, 58-60, 66-68, 78-80, 86-87, 93-95, 101-104, 110-113, 119-122, 127-129, 134-136, 140-142, 194
   strength of, 12-15
   strong, 12-14, 34-35
   strong enough, **ix**, 33, 37, 56-57, 64-65, 71, 77, 84, 91-92, 100, 108-110, 117-119, 125-126, 133, 138-139
   weak
      definition of, 6
      impact of, 6, 12-14, 33, 191-192
      why focus on, 25
listening, 45, 62, 67, *see communication*
lists, defined, 141,

magical thinking, 118, 180
material constipation, 112
mental clutter, *see clutter, mental*
mental health, defined, 98
message, 62, *see communication*
milestones, 45, 60, 90, *see goal-setting*

INDEX

mindfulness, vii, viii, 45, 226
mindset, *see attitude*
mission, 90, *see goal-setting*
mode, 62, *see communication*
Morgenstern, Julie, 95
motivation, defined, 83
Myers-Briggs Type Indicator, 230
myths, *see Productivity Myths*

National Association of Productivity and Organizing Professionals, 169
neat, 111
needs, ix, 4, 24, 40, 45, 55, 87, 89, 90, 100, 112, 161, 162, 179, 180, 192, 203, 205-207 *see goal-setting, secondary gains*

objectives, 90, *see goal-setting*
objects, defined, 107-108, *see Organization of Objects/Data link*
open-door policy, 59
order, xi, 45, 106, 111, 170, 226
Orfalea, Paul, 172
Organization of Objects/Data link, xi, 2, 4-5, 7-8, 45, 72, 106-114, 169-174, 221 *see Productivity Chain*
    story about, 8, 17, 30, 47, 110, 139-140, 212
organizational goals, 90, *see goal-setting*
organizational support, 132
organizing, conventional, ix, x, 1-2, 7-9, 42, 47, 106-107, 169-174
over-committment, 45, 56, 167
oversight, 78-79, 215

Pareto Principle, 167
peace of mind, xiii, xvi, 11, 14, 38, 41, 57, 83, 87, 149, 153, 156
people management, 45, 226
perfectionism, 41, 45, 84, 88, 145, 172, 174, 214, 226
personality, 45, 132, 135-136, 226
perspective, x, xiii, xvi, 6, 9, 10, 16, 18-25, 35, 43, 87, 100-101
physical health, defined, 97
Planning link, xi, 2, 4-5, 45, 72, 115-123, 176, 185, 222
    see Productivity Chain
    story about, 26, 30, 34, 47-48, 119, 162
power, x, 6, 21-23, 31-32, 37-38, 40-41, 57, 66, 86, 149, 156, 183, 193, 198-202, 209
    of links, 55, 61, 70, 76, 82, 89, 97, 106, 115, 124, 131, 137, 149
    misuses of, 40-41, 196-197
Power Chain, 10, 37-42, 209-211, *see Chain Reaction, Productivity Chain*
    productivity benefits of, 39
prioritization, 90-91, *see Goal-setting/ Prioritization link*
problem, x, xii, 1-3, 6-7, 18-22, 199
    definition/labeling, 19-21
    upside of, 203-207
    why that word, 18
problem-solving, 45, 71, 227
processing modalities, 45, 132, 227
procrastination, xii, 41, 45, 54, 117, 166, 171, 205, 227
productivity, defined, 7, 38-39, 121, 165, 188-190
Productivity Chain
    explanation of, x-xiii, 1-45
    graphics, 2, 5, 45
    impact on teams, 191-192
    see
    Boundary-setting link
    Communication/Relationships link
    Decision-making link
    Delegation link
    Drive link
    Goal-setting/Prioritization link
    Health link
    Organization of Objects/Data link
    Planning link
    Reinvention link
    Resources link
    Task/Project Management link
Productivity Chain Analysis, 24-32, 42, 220-222 *see Instant Reframe, Self-Assessment, Situation Analysis*
Productivity Myths, 22, 149-212
Professional Organizer, ix, 109
projects,
    defined, 138
    planning/breakdown, 115, 117-121
    prioritized, 91

project management, traditional, 45, 138
purpose, 90, *see goal-setting*

recipients, 62, *see communication*
reframing, 21-22, 149, 220-222, *see Instant Reframe*
Reinvention link, viii, xi, 2, 4-5, 45, 124-130, 188-190, 205-207, 222
    see Productivity Chain
    story about, 29, 47, 49, 126-129
relationships, 61, 63-64, *see Communication/Relationships link*
resentment, 41, 193, 198, 203-207, 227
Resources link, viii, xi, 2, 4-5, 45, 64, 131-136, 222, *see Productivity Chain*
    story about, 29, 32, 133-134
respect, 4, 39, 42, 56-57, 62-64, 66-68, 86, 117, 120, 131, 199, 203
responsibility, 21-23, 31, 41, 196-202, 199
results, defined, 7
review, 142, *see lists*
roles, 57, 91

scheduling, 115-123, *see Planning link*
secondary gains, 203-207
Self-Assessment, Productivity Chain, 24-28, *see Productivity Chain Analysis*
simplicity, 103, 112-113, 121-122
Situation Analysis, 24-25, 28-31, *see Productivity Chain Analysis*
skills, job-related, 132
SMARTT goals, 94, *see goals*
social health, defined, 98
solution, 6, 33-36, 199
spiritual health, defined, 98
standardization, 117
strategizing, 117

stress, xi, xvi, 1, 9, 17, 25, 27, 39, 41, 45, 49, 98-99, 102-103, 114, 133, 146, 154, 172, 180, 206, 214, 220
strong enough, *see link, strong enough*
Swonk, Diane, 172
symptoms, 19, 24, 31

Take Action, 7, 19, 22, 27, 31, 35, 54, 68, 87, 107, 113, 178, *see Exercises*
talent, 132, 228
tasks,
    defined, 116, 137-138
    prioritized, 91
Task/Project Management link, xi, 2, 4-5, 16, 34, 45, 72, 87, 137-143, 176, 206-207, 222
    see Productivity Chain
    story about, 30, 34
teamwork, 63, 228
Three O's, 99, *see balance*
Time
    just enough, 162-163, 179
    limits of, ix, 178-181
    management, ix, 42, 45, 71, 228
timing, 62, *see communication*
to-do's, defined, 137
tools, defined, 131
Tracy, Brian, 95
traumatic brain injury, 224
triage, 156
Twelve Links, *see Productivity Chain*

values, ix, 4, 5, 41, 45, 55, 90, 161
    see goal-setting
victim, 22, 198
vision, 90, *see goal-setting*

workaholism, 166, 228
work ethic, 85, 164-165, 228

Made in the USA
Las Vegas, NV
06 October 2021